FIRST
FUN
DICTIONARY

First published in 2001 by Miles Kelly Publishing Ltd
Bardfield Centre
Great Bardfield
Essex, U.K., CM7 4SL

This edition published by Barnes & Noble, Inc.

2 4 6 8 10 9 7 5 3 1

Author
Cindy Leaney

Editorial Director
Anne Marshall

Project Management
Belinda Gallagher

Editorial Assistant
Mark Darling

Copy Editor
Margaret Berrill

Proofreader
Lynn Bresler

Designer
Cathy May

Library of Congress Cataloging-in-Publication Data on file at the
Library of Congress.

2003 Barnes & Noble Books

ISBN 0-7607-4768-7

Printed and bound in China

FIRST FUN DICTIONARY

Cindy Leaney

BARNES
&NOBLE
BOOKS
NEW YORK

How to use your dictionary

Your dictionary is a book about words. It shows you how to spell words and explains what they mean. It also tells you how to use them. Many words will be familiar—the kind you use every day. Some will be new ones you are just beginning to learn. All are clearly explained. As you use your book you will find fun things to do and look at. Each letter of the alphabet has its own cartoon, and throughout the book there are puzzles, word games, and fact panels.

Cartoons
When a new letter starts, look for the fun cartoons at the top of the page. These are brightly colored scenes. See how many different things you can find starting with the same letter in each cartoon.

Did you know?
Look for the orange panels to find out interesting facts about the words in your book.

kaleidoscope to kind

Kk

kaleidoscope
a tube with pictures or pieces of colored glass or plastic at one end that you look through and turn to see changing patterns
The kaleidoscope was invented in 1816.

pattern

colored glass

▼ **kaleidoscope**

tube can be turned to make patterns

kangaroo
an Australian animal that keeps its young in a pouch on the front of its body
Kangaroos have big, strong back legs. ◀ **kangaroos**

karate
a Japanese fighting sport
In karate, you fight using your hands and feet.
◀ **karate**

keep (keeping, kept)
1 to continue to have something
You can keep the library books for two weeks.
2 to continue to do something
Don't keep staring at that man.
3 to have something in a certain place
The paints and crayons are kept on the shelf.

kettle
a container or machine for boiling water
I'll put the kettle on and make some tea.

key
1 a special piece of metal used to open a lock
Turn the key to the right.
2 one of the parts of a computer or piano that you press with your fingers
Type the file name and then press the "enter" key.
3 a set of answers or an explanation of symbols
There is a key at the back of the book.
◀ **key**

keyboard
the set of keys on a computer or a piano that you press to type or make a sound
This is a special keyboard with letters and pictures.

▲ **keyboard**

kick (kicking, kicked)
to swing your foot at something
Kick it into the net!

▲ **kick**

kill (killing, killed)
to cause someone or something to die
Some weeds kill other plants.

kind
helpful, pleasant, and thoughtful
It's very kind of you to think of me.

king to knot

king
a royal man who rules a country
Do you think the prince will become king? ◀ **king**

from the kitchen.

kite
a toy made of light wood and cloth, paper, or plastic that you fly at the end of a long string
I like to fly my kite on windy days.

· Did you know? ·
Henry VIII was king of England from 1509 to 1547. He had six wives.

kiss (kissing, kissed)
to touch someone else with your lips
Mom kissed us all good night.

kitchen
the room in a house for preparing food
There are good smells coming

· Puzzle time ·
How many kitchen things can you find in this word puzzle?
sinkovencupboardtable chairshelfcupandsaucer

answer
8

kitten
a baby cat

Our cat has two kittens. ◀ **kittens**

knee
the part of your leg that bends
If you lift something heavy, you should bend your knees.

knife (knives)
a tool with a blade for cutting things into pieces
Put the knife to the right of your plate.

▲ **knife**

knit (knitting, knitted)
to join wool together with long metal sticks
Jodie can knit. ▼ **knitting**

◀ **kite**

knock (knocking, knocked)
to hit something to make a noise
Knock on the back door.

knot
the place where two pieces of string or rope are tied together
There are many different ways to tie knots.

▲ **knot**

Alphabetical order
The words in this book are in alphabetical order. This means that all words beginning with A are grouped together, and so on. The colored band along the bottom of every page will tell you which letter of the alphabet you are looking at.

Puzzle time
These are fun things to do and give you a chance to play with words. This helps you learn and remember them. All puzzle time activities are in green panels. These could be things like finding missing letters, word scrambles, matching pictures with words, or spot-the-difference games.

Entries

There are more than 1,300 entries in your book. These are the words in **bold** type that you look up. For example, if you want to look up the word **plan**, go to the part of the book where the words begin with **p**. Look for the words that begin with **pl**, until you find the word you want.

Definitions

Each entry is clearly explained, or defined.

Pp

place
where something is—the position, point, or other location
There is a special place, deep in the forest.

plain
1 one color; having no pattern or decoration
The curtains are plain green.
2 easy to understand
Can you tell me in plain English?
3 not fancy or complicated
It's a plain room, but very clean and neat.

plan
1 an idea about what will happen in the future
We have vacation plans.
2 a drawing of a room, building, or other space
We drew a plan for our perfect playground.

plan (planning, planned)
to think about what you want to do and how to do it
We're planning a party.

plane
an airplane
The plane took off from the airport on time.

planet
one of the very large, round objects that moves around the sun
There are nine planets in our solar system.

Pluto

Neptune

Uranus

Saturn

Jupiter

Earth

Mars

rcury

Venus

anets

plant
(planting, planted)
to put seeds or plants into the ground or in containers so that they will grow
Plant the seeds in early summer.

plant
a living thing that has roots, leaves, and seeds and can make its own food
Water the plant every day.

plaster
a very thick paste that hardens when it dries
Plaster is used to cover walls inside buildings.

plastic
a light material that is made from chemicals
The bucket is made of plastic.

plate
a flat dish to eat food from
Take the plates into the kitchen.

▲ plates

play
a story performed by actors in a theater or on the radio
The Tempest is a play full of magical things.

play (playing, played)
to do things that you like, such as games or sports
Let's play outside.

▲ play

playground
a place for children to play
There are swings and a slide at the playground.

please
a word to use when you are asking for something politely
Please wait here.

plenty
enough or more than enough
Have one of my sandwiches, I have plenty.

plow
a piece of equipment that farmers use to turn the soil before they plant
Modern plows can cut through the soil very quickly.

▲ plow

plug
1 a piece of plastic or rubber that stops water from going out of a sink or bathtub
Put the plug in the bathtub, then turn on the water.
2 a piece of plastic connected to an electrical wire that you put into a wall
Which one is the plug for the computer?

plumber
a person whose job is to fix water faucets and pipes
The plumber repaired the leak.

plus (pluses)
and; added to; the symbol +
Eleven plus six equals seventeen.

$11 + 6 = 17$ ◀ plus

pocket
a small, flat bag sewn into a piece of clothing or luggage
Put your key in your pocket.

poem
writing that uses words that sound good together. The words may rhyme
This poem is very funny.

·Puzzle time·
Here is a scrambled poem. Can you put each line in the correct order?
Hint—each line begins with a word that has a capital letter.

a. Roses red are
b. are blue Violets
c. sweet is Sugar
d. And are you so

d. And so are you
c. Sugar is sweet
b. Violets are blue
a. Roses are red
answers

a b c d e f g h i j k l m n o p q r s t u v w x y z **89**

Illustrations and photographs

These also help you understand the meaning of a word. Each illustration or photograph has its own label to tell you exactly what it is. Some of the illustrations are big, and they may have several labels to tell you what different areas of the illustration are called.

Different forms of a word

Some of the entries are followed by the same word in a different form. The plural form is used when there is more than one of something. Usually this just means adding an "s." If a plural is more complicated than this, for example, the plural of "**knife**" is "**knives**," it is shown after the entry in smaller type within brackets.

If an entry is a verb (doing word) other forms of the word will appear in the parentheses. For example, the verb **play** is followed by different endings, which appear in smaller type in parentheses—**playing**, **played**. These show you when the action is happening or has happened.

Example sentences

These sentences follow the definition in *italic* type. They show you how you can use the word.

Aa

above
1 in a higher place
Ann lives on the floor above us.
2 more than
Snow melts when the temperature is above 32 degrees.

accident
something that happens by chance
I dropped it by accident.

actor (actress, actresses)
a person who plays a part in a film or play
Charlie Chaplin was a famous actor.

▶ **actor**

add (adding, added)
1 to put something together with something else
Add the eggs, sugar, and chocolate.
2 to put numbers together to find the total
Add six and four to make ten.

adult
a grown-up, not a child
Only adults are allowed in the pool after 6:00 P.M.

▲ **adult**

adventure
an exciting experience
Taking the plane by myself was a real adventure.

advertisement
words or pictures in a newspaper or magazine, or on television or radio, about things for sale
I saw an advertisement for a new candy bar.

area
an area is a part of a place or a country
You will find restaurants in that area of the town.

afraid
a feeling that something bad is going to happen
Are you afraid of snakes or spiders?

afternoon
the part of the day between noon and the evening
Let's go shopping this afternoon.

again
to do something once more
Can you say that again?

age
the number of years someone has lived.
At what age can I learn to drive a car?

aircraft
machines that fly
Helicopters, airplanes, and gliders are kinds of aircraft.

airplane
a large machine, with wings and an engine, that flies
Sometimes airplanes fly over our house.

airport
a place where airplanes land and take off from
The airport is very busy.

▼ **airplane**

a b c d e f g h i j k l m

alarm

a machine that flashes or makes a noise as a warning
The burglar alarm is flashing!

alien

something strange that comes from another planet
E.T. is a friendly alien.

▼ **aliens**

alligator

an animal with a long tail and big teeth that lives around rivers and lakes
Alligators lay eggs.

▲ **alligators**

alphabet

letters in a special order that you use to write a language
The English alphabet starts with A and ends with Z.

a b c d e f g h i
j k l m n o p q r
s t u v w x y z

ambulance

a vehicle for taking people who are sick or hurt to and from the hospital
Cars pull over to one side when an ambulance is coming.

▲ **ambulance**

angry

a feeling that something is wrong or unfair
I am angry with you.

animal

a living thing that can move
Humans, fish, birds, and lizards are all animals.

·Puzzle time·

Which animal doesn't belong?

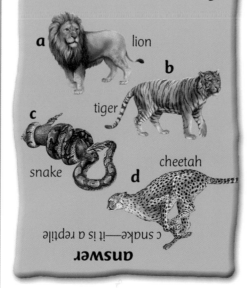

a lion
b tiger
c snake
d cheetah

answer
c snake—it is a reptile

ankle

part of the body between the leg and the foot that bends
I have twisted my ankle.
see also foot

▶ **ankles**

answer

1 something you say or write after a question
My answer is no.
2 the correct reply to a question, or the correct result to a problem.
That's the right answer!

answer (answering, answered)

1 to say or write something when asked a question
You must answer the questions.
2 to pick up the telephone or go to the door
Answer the door!

ant

an insect that lives in groups
There is a line of ants marching into the sugar bowl!
see also insect

▼ **ants**

appear (appearing, appeared)

1 to look or to seem
She appears to be much better.
2 to come into sight
Our sister suddenly appeared.

apple

a fruit that grows
on trees
*Apples are red,
yellow, or green.*
see also fruit

◀ **apple**

apricot

a small, fuzzy, yellow fruit
*I like dried apricots
on cereal.*

▲ **apricots**

apron

a piece of cloth that you put
on top of your clothes to keep
them clean.
*Put an apron on before you
open the paint.*

▲ **apron**

aquarium

a plastic or glass box filled
with water for keeping fish in
The fish swim in the aquarium.

·Puzzle time·

Can you untangle the lines to see
which fish has eaten the worm?

argue (arguing, argued)

to strongly disagree
Don't argue, it's not important.

arm

part of your body between
your shoulder and hand
*My right arm is stronger than
my left arm.*

armchair

a chair with places to rest
your arms
I like to read in an armchair.
see also chair

army

the people that fight for a
country on land
*The Roman army was very
powerful.*

arrest (arresting, arrested)

to take someone away and
guard them
The police arrested two people.

art

paintings, drawings, and
sculpture
There is an art show at school.

artist

a person who makes art
Picasso is a famous artist.

▲ **artist**

ask (asking, asked)

to say to someone you want
them to tell you something,
or do something for you
You should ask for help.

asleep
sleeping
Shhh, she is fast asleep.

▲ asleep

astronaut
a person who travels into space in a spacecraft
Astronauts sometimes spend months on a space station.

▲ astronaut

• Did you know? •
The first person to travel in space was Yuri Gagarin, a Russian astronaut, in 1961.

athlete
a person who plays a sport.
Athletes train every day.
see also sport

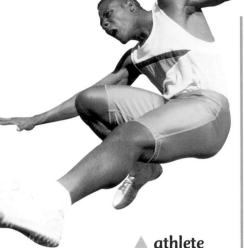
▲ athlete

attack (attacking, attacked)
to go at something in a violent way
Pirates attacked the ship.

aunt
the sister of your mother or father, the wife of your uncle
My aunt looks like my mother.
see also family

autograph
the name of a famous person, written by him or her
Can I have your autograph?

automatic
a machine that works by itself
The washing machine is automatic.

autumn (fall)
the time of year between summer and winter, also called fall
The leaves turn red in autumn.

▲ autumn

awake
not sleeping, not asleep
I tried to stay awake all night.

awful
very bad
This medicine tastes awful.

ax
a tool with a handle and a sharp piece of metal at the end that is used for chopping wood and cutting down trees
Dad uses an ax to chop wood.

▲ ax

Bb

baboon
a large monkey
Baboons are very noisy.

baby (babies)
a young child that has not yet learned to talk or walk
The baby's name is Alex.

▶ **baby**

back
1 part of your body behind you, between your shoulders and hips
I can swim on my back.
2 the part of something that is farthest from the front or from the way it is facing
The wires are at the back of the computer.

backward, backwards
the direction opposite to the way something is facing
Take four steps backward.

bacon
meat from a pig
We have bacon and eggs for breakfast.

bad (worse, worst)
not good or pleasant
The weather is very bad.

badge
a piece of metal, plastic, or cloth that you wear to show what your job is or that you belong to a group
The sheriff wore a silver badge.

badger
an animal with black and white fur that lives underground
There is a family of badgers living in the woods.

▼ **badger**

·Puzzle time·

These words are written backwards. Can you tell what they say?

tahw a ynnuf yaw ot etirw sdrow

answer
what a funny way to write words

badly
not done well
He played the piano badly.

badminton
a game like tennis that is played with rackets and a small object with feathers
We play badminton at the sports center.

▼ **badminton**

racket

shuttlecock

bag
a container made of plastic, paper, cloth, or leather
Put the vegetables into one bag.

baggy
loose, not tight
I like baggy sweaters.

bake (baking, baked)
to cook food in an oven
Bake the cake for 40 minutes.

balcony
an area outside a window where you can sit or stand
You can see the beach from the balcony.

bald
without hair
My dad is going bald.

ball
an object that you throw, hit, or kick in games
Throw the ball in the air.

ballet
a type of dancing that tells a story with no words
Swan Lake is a very famous ballet.

◀ **ballet**

balloon
a rubber bag filled with air that is used as a decoration
We had balloons at the party.

•Puzzle time•

a. How many red balloons can you see?
b. How many blue balloons can you see?
c. How many purple balloons can you see?

answers
a.3 b.3 c.2

banana
a long, curved yellow fruit
I like bananas with my cereal.

▲ **bananas**

bang
a sudden, loud noise
The door shut with a bang.

bank
1 a place to keep money
There is a bank in the town.
2 the land alongside a river
People sit on the bank and fish.

barn
a large farm building for keeping animals or crops
The cows are in the barn.

see also farm

▲ **barn**

baseball
a game played by two teams who try to get points by hitting a ball and running around the four corners of a diamond
There are nine players on a baseball team.

basket
a container made of thin strips, to hold or carry things
Put the bread in the basket.

basketball
a game played by two teams who try to get points by throwing a ball through a round net
Basketball is a fast game.

▼ **basketball**

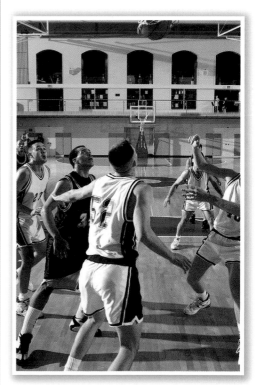

bat

1 a small animal that usually flies at night
Bats use sound to help them move around.
2 the stick used to hit a ball in games such as baseball and cricket
Baseball bats are round, cricket bats are flat.

▶ **bat**

bath

washing yourself in a long container filled with water
I like taking a warm bath.

beach (beaches)

the land next to the ocean
We had a picnic on the sandy beach.

▲ **beach**

bean

the seed of a climbing plant that is eaten as food
I like hot dogs and baked beans.

▶ **beans**

bear

a large, strong wild animal that is covered in fur
Bears have strong, sharp claws.

▲ **polar bear**

beard

hair that grows on a man's chin and cheeks
My dad has a beard.

beautiful

very pleasant or pretty
Roses are beautiful flowers.

bed

a piece of furniture for sleeping on
There are two beds in my room.

bee

a yellow and black striped insect
Bees live in a nest called a hive.
see also insect

▲ **bee**

begin (beginning, began)

to start
Begin at the top of the page.

behind

at the back of someone or something
She's hiding behind that fence.

bell

▼ **bell**

1 a hollow metal object that makes a sound when hit
Press the bell for service.
2 a machine that makes a ringing sound
The bell rings at 3:15 P.M.

•Puzzle time•

Untangle the bees to see which one gets home.

below

in a lower place than something else
The gym is on the floor below.

belt

a piece of clothing that you wear around your waist
Belts can be made of leather, cloth, or plastic.

◀ **belt**

bench (benches)

a seat for two or more people to sit on
Wait on the bench.

see also chair

▲ **bench**

better (best)

more suitable or pleasing
The new game is better than the last one.

between

in a place or time that separates two things or people
She is sitting between her brother and sister.

beyond

after a place
It's just beyond the next hill.

bicycle (bike)

a machine with two wheels that you sit on and move by pushing on pedals to make the wheels go around
I'm asking for a new bicycle for my birthday.

seat

wheel

handlebar

spoke

chain

pedal

▲ **bicycle**

•Puzzle time•

Can you unscramble the names of these birds ?

a. fupfin

b. eglae

c. eapccko

d. llguase

answers
a. puffin b. eagle
c. peacock d. seagull

big (bigger, biggest)

1 large, not small
The sweatshirt is too big.
2 important
Tomorrow is a big day.

bike

You can ride on a bike.

see also bicycle

bird

an animal that has wings and feathers and lays eggs
Most birds can fly.

▶ **bird**

binoculars
an instrument that you look through to make things far away seem nearer
Look through these binoculars.

birthday
the day of the year on which a person was born
When is your birthday?

bite (biting, bit, bitten)
to cut into something with your teeth
Take a bite of the apple.

▲ **bite**

bitter
having a strong, sharp taste, such as coffee
Add more sugar, it tastes bitter.

blanket
a piece of material on a bed that you use to keep warm
There's a blanket on the bed.

blind
not able to see
Talking books are made for blind people.

blister
a raised piece of skin, filled with liquid, caused by burning or rubbing
I have a blister on my foot.

blizzard
a very heavy snowstorm
People shouldn't drive in a blizzard.
see also weather

blood
the liquid that your heart pumps through your body
Blood looks very red.

bloom (blooming, bloomed)
to open out into a flower
There are flowers blooming all over the garden.

blow (blowing, blew)
to push air out of your mouth.
It's fun to blow bubbles!

▼ **blow**

boat
a small ship
You get to the island by boat.

▲ **boat**

·Puzzle time·
Find four different types of boat in this word puzzle.

shipboatyachtferry
ship boat yacht ferry
answers

body (bodies)
1 all of a person
Skin covers your entire body.
2 a dead person
They covered the body with a blanket.

bone
a hard, white part under the skin of a person or animal
Your body has more than 200 bones.

▶ **bones**

book

1 sheets of paper with writing on them joined together for reading
This is a book about spiders.
2 sheets of paper joined together for writing on
Write your name on the cover of your notebook.

boot

1 a shoe that covers your foot and ankle
Wear your boots in the rain.

▶ **boots**

bored

not interested
I'm bored, let's play a game.

born

starting life
When were you born?

borrow (borrowing, borrowed)

to have something that belongs to another person and return it to them
You can borrow the books for two weeks.
see also lend

bottle

a tall container for storing liquid
I have a water bottle on my bike.

▶ **bottles**

bottom

the lowest part of something
The number is at the bottom of the page.

bounce (bouncing, bounced)

1 to move back quickly after hitting or falling on something
Bounce on the trampoline.
2 to throw something against something so that it moves back quickly
Bounce the ball against the wall.

bow

1 a knot with loops
Tie a bow on top of the present.
2 a long, thin stick with string for shooting arrows or playing an instrument
You play the violin with a bow.

bow (bowing, bowed)

to bend your body or your head to show respect
People bowed to the king.

bowl

a deep, curved dish
You eat cereal out of a bowl.
see also dish

box (boxes)

a container with four sides
Keep the crayons in a box.

boxing

the sport of fighting with closed hands
There is a boxing match on TV.

boy

a male child or a young man
There are two boys in their family.

bracelet

a piece of jewelry worn around the wrist
My bracelet has my name on it.
see also jewelry

▲ **bracelet**

Braille

a type of printing that uses raised bumps
Blind people read Braille.

◀ **Braille**

controls thoughts and actions

controls body functions, emotions, and smell

controls muscles

controls balance

controls anger

controls learning and memory

▲ **brain**

brain
the part of your body inside your head that you use for thinking, feeling, and moving
When you touch something hot, nerves send a message to your brain and you pull your hand away.

branch
the part of a tree that grows out from the trunk
Leaves, flowers, and fruit grow on branches.

bread
a type of food made with flour, water, and yeast
Have some bread and butter.

break (breaking, broke, broken)
to make something separate into two or more pieces
Carry the glass carefully so that you don't drop and break it.

breakfast
the first meal of the day
We had cereal for breakfast.

breeze
a light wind
There's a nice breeze blowing.

brick
a block of baked clay used for building
The wall is made of bricks.

bridge
a structure that joins two sides, such as a road or a river
There is a bridge over the river.

▲ **bridge**

bright
1 full of light
It's a bright, sunny day.
2 strong and easy to see
Wear bright colors when you go into the woods.
3 smart, clever
That's a bright idea.

brilliant
1 very bright and strong
Sirius is one of the most brilliant stars in the sky.
2 very good at doing something
She's a brilliant scientist.

bring (bringing, brought)
to take something with you
Come over, and bring one of your friends.

broccoli
a green vegetable
Let's have some broccoli with dinner.

broom
a brush with a handle
Sweep the floor with a broom.

brother
a boy or a man who has the same parents as another person
Nadia has two brothers.
see also family

brush (brushes)

a tool with stiff hairs fastened to a handle that is used for sweeping, painting, cleaning, or smoothing
Here is a brush to paint with.

•Puzzle time•

Which one doesn't belong?

a

b

c

d

answer
c. broom

bucket

a round, open container with a handle
Put the water in a bucket.

build (building, built)

to make something, such as a house, by putting pieces together
There are plans to build a new school next year.

building

a place with a roof and walls
The Taj Mahal is a building in India.

▲ **building**

bull

a male cow, elephant, or whale
There's a bull running loose in that field.

burglar

a person who goes into buildings to steal things
A burglar stole the money.

burn (burning, burned, burnt)

1 to be alight or on fire
The candles are burning.
2 to hurt or destroy something with fire
The shed burned down.

bus (buses)

a large vehicle that carries passengers
The bus stops on our street.

bush (bushes)

a plant like a small tree
Blackberries grow on bushes.

butter

a yellow food that is made from milk
Spread butter on the bread.

butterfly (butterflies)

an insect with large wings
Butterflies drink from flowers.
see also cocoon

▶ **butterfly**

button

a small, round object that you push through a hole to fasten clothes
There are five buttons on my shirt.

buy (buying, bought)

to get something by paying money for it
Let's buy this book.

Cc

cabbage
a large vegetable with thick, round leaves
Cabbages can be green, white, or red.

► **cabbage**

cabin
1 a small house made of wood, usually in the country.
The cabin is halfway up the mountain.
2 the place where the passengers sit inside an airplane
The pilot walked back through the cabin.
3 a small room to sleep in on a ship
The cabin has two beds.

cactus (cactuses, cacti)
a plant that grows in hot, dry places that has needles instead of leaves
The needles on a cactus are sharp.

► **cactus**

café
a place that serves drinks and simple meals
That café has tables outside.

•Puzzle time•
Use the code to find out what they ordered at the café:

A	B	C	D	E	F	G	H	I	J
1	2	3	4	5	6	7	8	9	10

K	L	M	N	O	P	Q	R
11	12	13	14	15	16	17	18

S	T	U	V	W	X	Y	Z
19	20	21	22	23	24	25	26

16/9/26/26/1
19/1/12/1/4

answer
pizza and salad

cage
a room or box made of bars to keep animals or birds in
He keeps his pet mouse in a cage.

cake
a sweet food made of flour, sugar, and eggs that is baked in an oven
Let's make a chocolate cake.

calendar
a special chart that shows the days, weeks, and months of the year
We wrote everyone's birthday on the calendar in our classroom.

calf (calves) ▲ calf
1 a baby cow, elephant, or whale
The calf is two days old.
2 the back part of your leg between your ankle and knee.
I pulled a muscle in my calf when I was playing tennis.
see also leg

call (calling, called)
1 to shout or say something in a loud voice
Dad usually calls us in for dinner at six o'clock.
2 to telephone
Call me as soon as you get home.
3 to give someone or something a name
They called the baby girl Joanne.

▼ **camel**

camel
a large animal with one or two humps that can carry heavy loads
A camel can go without water for a long time.

camera
a piece of equipment used for taking photographs or filming
You get a digital camera free with this computer.

▲ **camera**

camp
a place where people stay in tents
The camp is over the hill.

camp (camping, camped)
to stay in a tent
Every summer, the scouts camp in this field.

can ▶ **can**
a metal container
We collected cans of food for charity.

can (could)
1 to be able to do something
Aziz can use the Internet.
2 to be allowed to do something
We can come to your party.
see also may

candle
a stick of wax with a string through it that you burn for light
There are nine candles on her birthday cake.

▲ **candle**

captain
1 someone who leads a team
Who is captain of the football team this year?
2 a person who is in charge of a ship or a plane
The captain says the flight will take two hours.

capture (captures, capturing, captured)
when you take a person, animal, or place by force
The police captured the thieves.

▼ **car**

trunk   roof   windshield
wheel   hood

car
a machine on wheels that has an engine and that people can ride in
There is a car in the driveway.

▶ **card**

card
1 a piece of stiff paper with words and a picture that you give or send someone
Peter gave me a birthday card.
2 a piece of stiff paper or plastic that you use to buy things or to identify yourself
I have a library card.
3 a piece of stiff paper with pictures and numbers that you use to play games
Give each player seven cards.

cardboard
thick, stiff paper
Use a piece of cardboard to make a sign.

cardigan
a piece of clothing like a sweater with buttons down the front
Wear a cardigan if it's cold.

careful (carefully)
paying attention to what you are doing so that you don't make a mistake
Be careful! That knife is sharp.

carpet
a thick cover for the floor
The carpet in my room is blue.

carrot
a long, orange vegetable that grows under the ground
Raw carrots are very good for you.

▲ carrots

carry (carrying, carried)
to move something from one place to another
Can you help me carry this?

cassette
a plastic box with a tape inside it for recording or playing back sound or video
Put the cassette into the machine and press "play."

castle
a large, strong building with thick walls
Castles were built to keep the people inside safe from their enemies.

cat
a small, furry animal with a long tail and sharp claws
My cat likes to climb trees.

▶ cat

•Puzzle time•

The "t" in castle is silent—you don't pronounce it when you say the word.
Each of these words has a silent letter. Do you know which ones are silent?

**calf   island   knee
knife   leopard**

Hint—you can look the words up in this dictionary if you don't know what they mean.

answers
calf island knee knife leopard

1. battlements
defensive areas on top of castle walls
2. gatehouse
the towers and gates that guard the entrance to a castle
3. great hall
a big business room inside a castle, sometimes used for feasting
4. portcullis
a heavy metal fence that seals off the castle gateway
5. tower
a tall building from which enemies can be seen

catch (catching, caught)
1 to get hold of something
Catch the ball!
2 to get an illness
People often catch cold in the winter.
3 to get on a bus, train, plane, or ferry and go somewhere
We usually catch the bus to the airport.

Inside a castle

caterpillar

an animal, like a worm with legs, that turns into a butterfly or a moth
Caterpillars eat leaves.

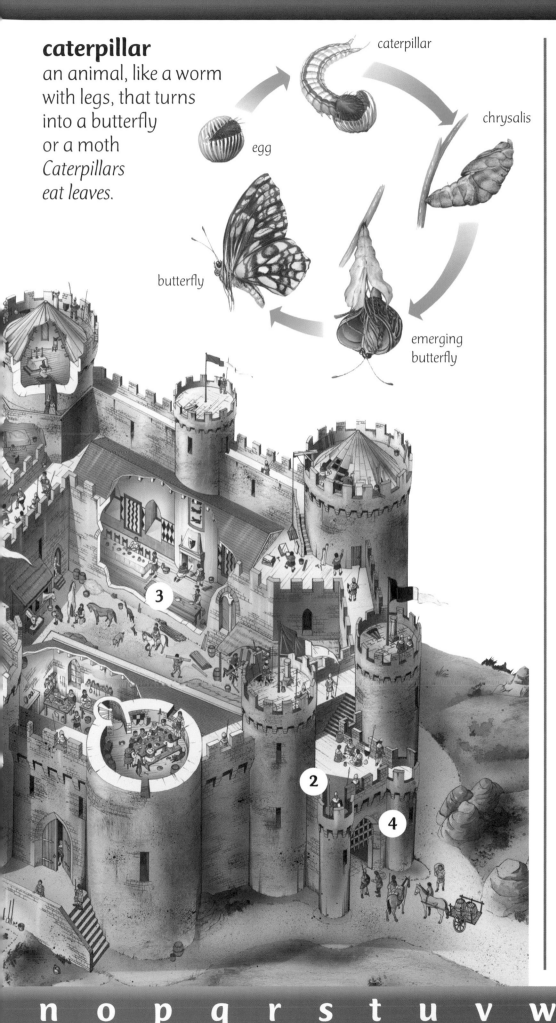

caterpillar

chrysalis

egg

butterfly

emerging butterfly

cave

a hole in a mountainside or under the ground.
Caves are usually dark.

CD (CDs, compact disc)

a circular piece of plastic for storing sound
Let's play a CD.

▶ CD

CD-ROM (CD-ROMs, compact disc read-only memory)

a circular piece of plastic for storing information to be used by a computer
CD-ROMs hold lots of information.

celery

a vegetable that is often used in salads
Celery is crunchy.

cereal

a breakfast food that is made from plants such as wheat, oats, and rice.
Pour some milk on the cereal.

n o p q r s t u v w x y z

chair
a piece of furniture for sitting on
Pull your chair close to the desk.

◄ **chair**

chalk
a soft, white rock
We used colored chalk to draw the picture.

▼ **chameleon**

chameleon
a lizard that changes color so its skin matches the things around it
Chameleons eat flies.

change (changing, changed)
1 to become different or to make something different
You haven't changed at all!
2 to put on different clothes
I'll be downstairs as soon as I've changed.

cheap (cheaper, cheapest)
not expensive
This watch is cheap, but it is well-made.

cheese
a food that is made from milk
Cheese tastes very good.

cherry (cherries)
a small, round, reddish fruit that has a pit in the center
We'll have cherry pie.

▲ **cherries**

chest
1 the part of your body between your neck and your stomach
Place the belt across your chest.
2 a strong box with a top that locks
The chest was filled with gold!

chicken
a farm bird that is kept for eggs and meat
Chickens can't fly very far.

▲ **chicken**

child (children)
1 a young person
Admission is free for children.
2 someone's son or daughter
They love all their children.

chimney
an opening over a fireplace that takes smoke out through the roof of a building
The chimney is filled with soot.

chin
▲ **chimneys**
part of the face under the mouth
His beard hides his chin.
see also face

chips
thin slices of potato fried until they are very crisp
I had chips with my sandwich.

chocolate
a sweet food made from cocoa beans
Would you like some chocolate?

Christmas
a Christian holiday
Where are you spending Christmas?
see also holiday

church (churches)
the place where Christians meet to worship
The church is full of flowers.

circle
a flat, perfectly round shape
Draw a circle on this page.

circus (circuses)
a show with people and animals, held in a big tent
The circus is in town!

Did you know?

Circuses are hundreds of years old. The first modern circus began in England in 1768, and involved horseback riding and live music. Today, modern circuses show breathtaking tricks and stunts.

city (cities)
a large town
It is a big, busy city.   ▼ **city**

clap (clapping, clapped)
to make a loud sound by hitting the palms of your hands together
The actors bowed, and we clapped louder.

class (classes)
1 a group of people who learn together
We're in the same class.
2 a group of things or animals that are the same
People belong to the class of animals called mammals.

claw
a sharp, hard part of an animal's foot
Cats have sharp claws.

clean (cleaning, cleaned)
to make something tidy, to take dirt away
Clean up your room!

clean
not dirty
The car is clean and shiny.

clear
1 easy to understand, hear, or read
The instructions are clear.
2 easy to see through
You can see the fish swimming in the clear water.

click (clicking, clicked)
a short, sharp sound
The switch made a click when she pressed it.

◀ **circus**

cliff

the side of a rock or mountain
The road runs along a cliff.

▲ cliff

climb (climbing, climbed)

to move upward
She climbed to the top.

▶ climb

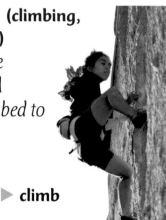

clock

a machine that tells the time
The clock said 5:55 A.M.

▲ clock

close (closing, closed)

to shut
Close the window, I'm cold.

close

near
The hotel is close to the beach.

cloth

1 a soft material
The chair is covered in cloth.
2 a piece of cloth for a special purpose
Clean the table with a damp cloth.

clothes

things that people wear
Shirts, jeans, and skirts are all clothes.

cloud

a white or gray object in the sky that is made of tiny drops of water
It's a beautiful day, with just a few small clouds.

clown

someone who makes people laugh
Harry is our class clown.

▶ clown

coast

the land next to the ocean
The village is on the coast.

coat

a piece of clothing you wear over your clothes to stay warm or keep the rain off
This is a warm coat.

coconut

the nut of the palm tree
Coconuts have delicious juice.

cocoon

the bag around an insect that protects it while it is growing
The cocoon broke open, and a butterfly flew out.
see also butterfly and caterpillar

◀ cocoon

coffee

the brown beans of a plant, or a hot drink made from them
Do you want coffee or tea?

coin

a piece of money that is made of metal
They keep coins from the countries they visit.

cold

not warm or hot
Brrr—this water is very cold.

collect (collecting, collected)
to put things together in one place
Some people collect coins, others collect stamps.

color
blue, green, red, and yellow
What color is your jacket?

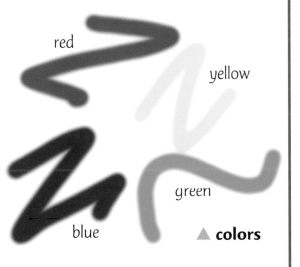

red

yellow

green

blue

▲ **colors**

color (coloring, colored)
to make something a color with paint, crayons, or ink
We colored the picture.

comb
an object with teeth for making your hair neat
You shouldn't let anyone else use your comb.

◄ **comb**

comic book
a magazine with pictures that tell a story
Comic books are often funny.

compass
an object that shows you what direction you are traveling in
If you can read a compass, you can find the treasure!

▲ **compass**

competition
a test to see who is best at something
There was a singing competition on the radio.

complain (complaining, complained)
to say that something is wrong and you are not happy about it
He complained to the waiter.

computer
a machine for storing information and doing jobs such as math and writing letters
You can play games on computers.

▲ **computer**

confused
a feeling of not being sure
I was confused by the question.

container
something that holds something else inside it
Jars, cans, and boxes are all different kinds of containers.

cook (cooking, cooked)
to make food hot so that it can be eaten
Ahmed is cooking dinner for us.

cookie
a dry, flat, sweet cake that is usually round
We baked oatmeal cookies.

cool
a little bit cold
The sun is hot, but there is a cool breeze.

copy (copying, copied)
to do something the same as something else
Copy the words on the board.

corn
a plant with large, yellow seeds
This corn is delicious.

▲ **corn**

cough (coughing, coughed)
to force air from your throat
*She's still coughing—give her
a drink of water.*

count (counting, counted)
to find out how many
*Count the children in the
playground.*

country (countries)
1 a place with its own
government
Which country do you live in?
2 away from cities and
towns.
*We live in a village in the
country.*

cousin
the child of your aunt
or uncle
Charlie is my cousin.
also look at family

cow (cows, cattle)
a large, female farm animal
that gives milk
Cows eat grass.

cowboy
a man who rides a horse and
takes care of cattle
*The cowboy tried to
ride the horse.*

▲ **cowboy**

crab
a sea animal that moves
sideways
and has
big claws
*Crabs
are good
to eat.*

▶ **crab**

crack
where something is broken
There's a crack in this cup.

crack (cracking, cracked)
to break something so that
a line appears on it
Just crack the shell.

crash (crashing, crashed)
1 to have an accident
The car crashed into a tree.
2 to make a loud noise
Hear the thunder crash!

crawl (crawling, crawled)
to move around on your
hands and knees
The baby is crawling.

crayon
a colored wax stick
Can I use your crayons?

creep (creeping, crept)
to move so that no one sees or
hears you
Oh! Don't creep up on me!

crime
something that is against
the law
Stealing the car was a crime.

crocodile
a large animal with a
long body, short legs, and
big teeth
Crocodiles live in rivers.

▼ **crocodile**

crooked

not straight
The fence is very crooked.

crop

plants that are grown to be eaten or used to make things
The weather is very important to farmers who grow crops.

cross

two lines that go over each other
There is a cross on the map where the treasure is hidden.

cross (crossing, crossed)

to go from one side of something to the other
Cross the street carefully.

crown

▼ **crown**

a metal circle that kings and queens wear on their heads
The queen and king are both wearing gold crowns.

cruel

not kind
He's a cruel king.

crumb

A small piece of something such as bread or cake
There are only crumbs left.

cry (crying, cried)

1 to make tears from your eyes, usually because you feel sad or are hurt
Sometimes you feel better after you cry.
2 to shout
"Help! Help!" they cried.

▶ **cry**

cucumber

a long, thin green vegetable that is used in salads
I'd like a cucumber and tomato salad.

cuddle (cuddling, cuddled)

to hold someone in your arms to show you care
Chloe cuddled her best friend to cheer her up.

◀ **cuddle**

cup

a container with a handle for drinking from
Put a tea bag in the cup, then add water.

cupboard

a piece of furniture for storing things
Please dry the dishes and put them in the cupboard.

curious

wanting to know or find out about something
Cats are very curious.

curl

something like hair or ribbon that is curved at the end
She has beautiful curls.

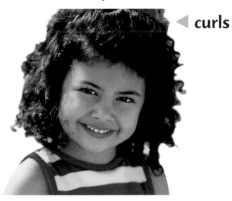
◀ **curls**

curtain

cloth that hangs across or over a window
Close the curtains at night.

cushion

a bag with soft material inside for sitting or lying on
He put a cushion on his chair.

cut (cutting, cut)

to remove something with a knife or scissors.
I'm going to get my hair cut.

Dd

daisy (daisies)
a flower with white petals and a yellow center
You can make a chain of daisies.

▼ daisies

dance (dancing, danced)
to move your body to music
This music is good to dance to.

dangerous
not safe
Playing with matches is dangerous.

dark
not light
We stay outside and play until it gets dark.

daughter
a female child
Her daughter's name is Amy.

•Puzzle time•
Can you match the pictures to the time of day?

a. eat breakfast **b.** play

c. do homework **d.** brush teeth

answers
a. morning b. afternoon
c. evening d. morning/night

day
1 a 24-hour period
We plan to stay here for three days.
2 from the time the sun rises until it sets
Bats do not usually fly during the day.

dead
not alive
This plant looks dead.

deaf
not able to hear
Many deaf people can read lips.

dear
1 a word to start a letter
Dear Aran, How are you?
2 much cared about
She's a very dear friend.

---

deep
a long way from the top to the bottom, or from the front to the back
I'm not afraid to swim in the deep end of the pool.

deer (deer)
an animal that lives in forests
Deer are gentle animals.

▲ deer

delicious
tasting very good
This ice cream is delicious.

delighted
very happy
I'm delighted with my new bike.

a b c d e f g h i j k l m

dentist

a person who cares for people's teeth
I go to the dentist twice a year.

▲ **dentist**

desert

a place where there is very little or no rain
Most deserts are hot.

▲ **desert**

desk

a piece of furniture that you sit at to read, write, or use a computer
There's a lamp on my desk.

dessert

sweet food that you eat at the end of a meal
What's for dessert?

▲ **dessert**

detective

a person who finds out information about a crime or another person
Some police officers are detectives.

diary

a book in which you write down what you have done and things that have happened
I write in my diary every night.

die (dice)

a cube with spots on each side that is used for playing games
It's your turn—throw the dice.

▲ **dice**

die (dying, died)

to stop living
Water the plant before it dies.

different

not the same
These two cookies look the same but they taste different.

difficult

not easy
I hope the spelling test isn't too difficult.

dig (digging, dug)

to make a hole in soil or to move it.
Big machines can dig faster than we can.

▲ **dig**

digital

1 showing information using numbers that can change
This is a digital watch.
2 storing information using only zero and one
Most music is digitally recorded these days.

dining room

the room in which you eat your meals.
The dining room is next to the kitchen in our house.

also look at house

dinner

the main evening meal
What's for dinner?

dinosaur

an animal that became extinct 65 million years ago
Tyrannosaurus Rex is one type of dinosaur.

also look at fossil

· Did you know? ·

The first record of dinosaur bones being found was less than 200 years ago. The bones were found in 1818 by Solomon Ellsworth, Jr., while he was digging a well at his home in Windsor, Connecticut.

Stegosaurus

Quetzalcoatlus

Ankylosaurus

▲ **dinosaurs**

Seismosaurus

dirty

not clean, messy
We put dirty clothes in the laundry basket.

disabled

a disabled person cannot use part of their body
This parking space is for disabled drivers only.

disappear (disappearing, disappeared)

to go out of sight or become impossible to find
The sun disappeared behind a cloud.

Stenonychosaurus

Pterodactyl

disco

a place or a party where people dance
There's a disco on Saturday.

discover (discovering, discovered)

to find or understand something for the first time
Alexander Fleming discovered penicillin, a type of medicine.

disease

a serious illness
Flu is a disease.

disguise

something that you wear to hide who you really are
Part of his disguise is a false beard.

▼ **disguise**

dish (dishes)

something like a bowl or plate, used for serving food
Please help me wash the dishes.

Diplodocus

disk
a piece of plastic for storing computer information
Save the file on a disk.

dive (diving, dived)
to go into water headfirst
I'm learning to dive.

▲ **dive**

Diwali
an important Hindu festival
Raj got a special gift for Diwali.
also look at holiday

dizzy
the feeling that things are turning around you or that you are going to fall
That ride makes me dizzy.

doctor
a person who cares for sick people or helps stop people from getting sick
Doctors work very hard.

▼ **doctor**

document
1 papers that contain official information
There are important old documents on display at the museum.
2 a piece of work that is saved in a file on a computer
You can attach a document to an e-mail.

dog
an animal that people keep as a pet
Our dog is a collie.

doll
a toy that looks like a person
Let's play with our dolls.

dolphin
a large animal that lives in the sea
There are places where you can swim with dolphins.

▲ **dolphin**

domino (dominoes)
a piece of black wood or plastic with white spots that is used to play games
Playing dominoes can help you with math!

▼ **donkey**

donkey
an animal that looks like a small horse with big ears
There are donkeys in that field.

door
something that you open and close to go into or out of a room, house, or car
Can you open the door for me?

down
1 toward a lower place
Get down off the ladder.
2 at a lower rate or speed
Prices are coming down.

dragon
an imaginary animal like a big lizard that breathes fire
The story is about a princess trapped in a dragon's cave.
also look at fairy tale

▶ **dragon**

dramatic
surprising or exciting
It's dramatic news.

draw (drawing, drew, drawn)
to make
a picture
*You can
draw very
well.*

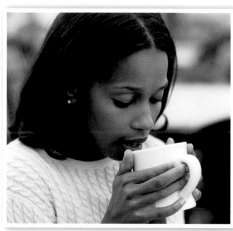

▶ draw

drawer
part of a piece of furniture
that slides in and out that is
used for storing things
Put the clothes in the drawer.

dream (dreaming, dreamed)
1 to think about or see things
in your sleep
*Last night I dreamed that I
could fly.*
2 to hope for something
We dream of being famous.

dress (dressing, dressed)
to put clothes on
Get dressed, we're ready to go.

dress (dresses)
a piece of clothing for girls
or women that has a top
and skirt
That's a beautiful dress.

drink
liquid food
*Coffee, tea, juice, and milk are
different kinds of drinks.*

▲ drink

drink (drinking, drank, drunk)
to take liquid into your mouth
and swallow it
Drink lots of water.

drive (driving, drove, driven)
to control a vehicle, like a car
My oldest brother can drive.

drop (dropping, dropped)
to fall or to let something fall
Don't drop that vase.

drum
a musical
instrument
that you hit with a
stick or your hand
He plays the drums.
also look at music

▲ drum

•Puzzle time•
How many things begin with
"d" in this picture?

dry
not wet
The laundry is almost dry.

duck
a bird with webbed feet that
lives near water
We feed bread to the ducks.

▼ duck

dungeon
a prison below ground in a
castle
*The prisoner was thrown
into the dungeon.*

DVD (digital versatile disk)
a circular piece of
plastic used for
storing and playing
music and films
Is the film on DVD?

Ee

eagle
a bird that hunts
for its food
*An eagle has sharp
claws and a beak.*

▶ **eagle**

ear
the part of your
body that you use to hear
My ears feel cold.

ear bones

eardrum

outer ear

▲ **ear**

early
before the normal time
I wake up early in the summer.

earn (earning, earned)
to get money for work
*I earn extra money for washing
the car.*

earring
a piece of jewelry that is worn
on the ear
*I wore my new earrings to
the party.*

▲ **earrings**

Earth (earth)
1 the planet we live on
*The Earth travels
around the sun.*
2 *Plants grow
in the earth.*

▶ **Earth**

earthquake
a strong shaking of the earth
*Earthquakes can cause serious
damage to buildings.*

Easter
a Christian holiday
also look at holiday

▲ **Easter eggs**

•Puzzle time•
How many Easter eggs
can you find?

easy
not difficult
This book is easy to read.

eat (eating, ate,
eaten)
to take food into your
mouth and swallow it
*I'm so hungry
I could eat
a horse!*

▲ **eating**

echo (echoes)
a sound that bounces off
something and can be heard
again
*There is a strong echo when you
shout into the cave.*

egg

1 an oval object with a shell that some animals lay, from which their babies hatch
There are four eggs in the nest.
2 an egg used as food
I can make fried eggs.

▶ **eggs**

elbow

where your arm bends
Ouch, I bumped my elbow.

electricity

power that is used to make lights and machines work
Lightning is a giant spark of electricity.

elephant

a large, wild animal with a long nose called a trunk
A baby elephant is called a calf.

▲ **elephant**

e-mail

messages sent by computer
I e-mail all my friends.

empty

with nothing inside
The box is empty.

end

to finish or stop
The film ends at 6:30 p.m.

enemy (enemies)

someone who does not like you, or wants to hurt you
We are enemies, not friends.

energy

strength or power
We're trying to save energy.

engine

1 a machine that makes something work
Engines are in the front of cars.
2 The part of a train that pulls the other cars
The steam engine is very noisy.

engine

enjoy (enjoying, enjoyed)

to like to do something
I enjoy playing tennis.

enormous

very, very big
Whales are enormous animals.

enough

as much as you need
There is enough for everyone.

enter (entering, entered)

1 to go into a place
The king entered the hall.
2 to put information into a computer
The names and addresses are entered in a file.

entrance

the way into a place
The entrance to the cave was very dark.

▼ **engine**

envelope

a paper cover for letters and cards
Put a stamp on the envelope.

▲ **envelopes**

environment

everything around us, such as land, air, or water
They live in a hot environment.

equal

the same as something else in number, size or amount
One pound is equal to 16 ounces.

•Puzzle time•

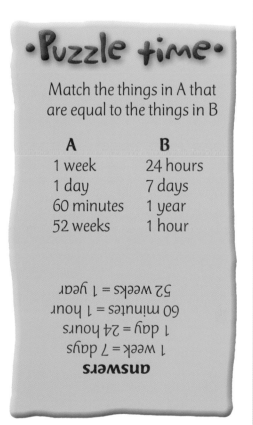

Match the things in A that are equal to the things in B

A	B
1 week	24 hours
1 day	7 days
60 minutes	1 year
52 weeks	1 hour

answers
1 week = 7 days
1 day = 24 hours
60 minutes = 1 hour
52 weeks = 1 year

equipment

things that are used to do something like work or sports
Our school has lots of new computer equipment.

escalator

a staircase that moves
We went up the escalator.

step
handrail
motor

▲ **escalator**

escape (escaping, escaped)

to leave a place that is dangerous or unpleasant
They escaped from the prison.

evening

the time of day between afternoon and nighttime
It starts to get dark in the evening.

▲ **evening**

excellent

very good
This is an excellent song.

excited

happy and interested in something
I am excited about tomorrow.

▼ **excited**

excuse

a reason you give for something that you have said or done
Her excuse for being late is that she overslept.

exercise

movements that you make to stay fit and healthy
Exercise keeps you healthy.

▼ **exercise**

exhibition

a show where people can look at things like paintings
There is an exhibition of our artwork at school.

exit

the way to leave a place
There is a light over the exit.

expensive

costing a lot
Jewelry can be very expensive to buy.

explain (explaining, explained)

to say what something means or why it has happened
Our teacher explained how the equipment worked.

explanation

what something means or why it happened
There is a good explanation for the accident.

explode (exploding, exploded)

to suddenly burst or blow up into small pieces
The fireworks exploded in the night sky.

explore (exploring, explored)

to look around a new place
We explored the cave.

▲ **explore**

explosion

the noise, smoke, and sometimes flames, that are made when something blows up into pieces
The explosion filled the air with clouds of smoke.

• Did you know? •

Your eyes measure only 1 inch (2.5 cm) across, but they can see things as far away as a star in space, and objects as tiny as a grain of sand.

▶ **parts of the eye**

extinct

no longer existing
The dodo is an extinct bird.

▼ **extinct**

dodo

•Puzzle time•

See how many different words you can make from

extinct

you should be able to make at least seven.

extra

more than is necessary
People are extra nice to you on your birthday.

eye

the part of the body that animals use to see
What color are your eyes?

retina

iris

pupil

lens

cornea

Ff

face

the front part of your head
*Your eyes, nose,
and mouth are
on your face.*

▶ **face**

factory

a place where things are
made in large numbers by
machines and people
*Hundreds of people work at
the car factory.*

faint

1 not strong or easy to
hear, see, or smell
*There is a faint smell
of smoke.*
2 feeling weak and
light-headed
I am so hungry I feel faint.

fair

1 good and reasonable
Their decision is fair.
2 light-colored
He has fair hair and blue eyes.
3 clear, sunny
*If the weather is fair, we'll go to
the beach.*

fairy (fairies)

a magical person with wings
*Tinkerbell is the name of the
fairy in* Peter Pan.

▼ **fairy**

fairy tale

a story for children about
magical things
Some fairy tales are very old.

▲ **fairy tale**

fake

not real
Her coat is fake fur.

fall (falling, fell, fallen)

to drop downward
*My little brother is learning to
walk, but he keeps falling down.*

false

not true, correct, or real
He gave a false name.

family (families)

a group of people who are
related to each other
*There are nine people in their
family.*

▼ **family**

famous

well-known
He's a famous football player.

fan

▼ **fan**

1 an object that
you hold in
your hand
and move, or
a machine that moves the air
to make it cooler
Sit in front of the fan and relax.
2 someone who likes a
particular thing or person
very much
My uncle is a Beatles fan.

far (faraway)
not near, a long distance away
I get letters from faraway places.

farm
a place where people grow crops and raise animals
Cows are kept on dairy farms.

▲ **farm**

fast
quick, not slow
Racing cars are very fast.

fat
1 weighing more than is good or normal
If you eat too much candy, you might get fat.
2 thick, big, or wide
Our teacher reads to us from a big, fat book.

father
a male parent
My father reads to me at night.

favorite
liked the best
Blue is my favorite color.

fax (faxes)
1 a document sent by a fax
There's a fax for you.
2 a machine you use to send documents over a telephone line
Use the fax to send a message.

fear (fearing, feared)
to have the feeling that something bad is going to happen or has happened
There is nothing to fear!

feast
a large, special meal to celebrate something
Thanksgiving dinner is a feast at our house.

feather
one of the soft, light things that cover a bird's body
Peacock feathers are beautiful colors.

◀ **feather**

feed (feeding, fed)
to give food to a person or an animal
It's fun to feed the chickens.

▼ **feed**

feel (feeling, felt)
1 to have an emotion
I feel happy to be home.
2 to touch or be touched by something
This sweater feels rough.

female
a woman, girl, or animal that can have babies when adult
Female sheep are called ewes.

fence

a wall made of wood or wire
There are plants growing next to our fence.

▼ **fence**

ferry (ferries)

a kind of ship
The ferry leaves at 8:00 a.m.

▲ **ferry**

few

1 not many
There are very few tickets left.
2 a small number
There are a few new messages.

field

a piece of land for growing crops, raising animals, or playing sports
There is a bull in that field.

fierce

angry and strong, or violent
Watchdogs can be very fierce.

▲ **fierce**

fight

when two or more people try to hurt each other
There is a fight outside.

file

1 information on a computer
Move your files to a new folder.
2 information about a person or subject kept for a reason
The doctor has files on all of the patients.

figure

1 a written number
Write all the figures down.
2 a person's shape
She saw the figure of a woman in the shadows.

fill (filling, filled)

to put things into something until it is full
Fill the vase with clean water for the flowers.

film

1 thin plastic that you put into a camera to take photographs
Digital cameras don't use film.
2 a movie
We saw a funny film.

▲ **film**

find (finding, found)

to see or get something that you are looking for
Can you find the answer?

•Puzzle time•

What is the missing letter?

fin_sh   f_ght
f_eld   f_erce

answers
finish fight field fierce

fine

1 very thin or in small pieces
The beach is covered with fine, white sand.
2 very good
They are fine singers.

finger

one of the five long parts on your hand
Your thumb is a finger.

▶ **fingers**

finish

(finishing, finished)
to end
Put your pencil down when you are finished.

fire

something that burns, giving out heat and flames
We lit a fire in the fireplace.

fire engine

a truck used to put out fires
Fire engines have flashing lights.

firework

small objects that explode into bright colors in the sky
The fireworks start after dark.

▼ **fireworks**

fish

an animal that lives underwater, has fins, and breathes through gills
There are seven fish in the tank.

▲ **fish**

fist

a closed hand
Can you guess which fist the coin is in?

fit

looking and feeling healthy
I feel very fit.

fix **(fixing, fixed)**

1 to repair
Dad is fixing the tractor.
2 to stick or attach
Fix the picture to the board.

▼ **fix**

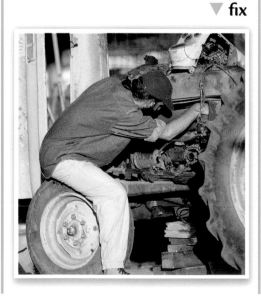

flag

a piece of cloth that is used as a signal, or the sign of a country.
The flag of the United States of America is called the Stars and Stripes.

◀ **flag**

flame

the burning gas from a fire or bright light from a candle
The flames were very bright.

▲ **flames**

flash

a bright burst of light
You can see the lightning flash.

flashlight

a light powered by batteries

flat

not bumpy or hilly, smooth
Put the paper flat on the table.

flavor

the taste of something
*Strawberry, chocolate, and
vanilla are flavors of ice cream*

flight

a journey in a plane
*The flight from New York to
London takes about five hours.*

float (floating, floated)

to stay on top of water or
another liquid, not to sink
It is easier to float if you relax.

▲ float

flood

a lot of water in a place that is
usually dry
*There were heavy rains and
then a flood.*

floor

the part of a room you stand
on
Everyone is sitting on the floor.

flower

the part of a plant that makes
the seeds or fruit
*Roses, pansies, daffodils, and
daisies are all flowers.*

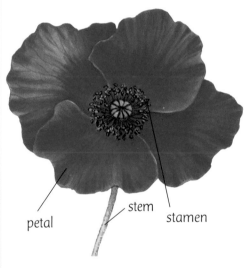

petal   stem   stamen

▲ flower

fly (flying, flew)

1 to move through the air
We flew at night.
2 a small insect
The fly was buzzing around.

▼ fly

fog

mist or cloud
You can't see very far in fog.

▲ fog

fold (folding, folded)

to turn or bend something
over on itself
Fold your clothes.

follow (following, followed)

to move after or behind
someone or something
Follow me!

food

something that people or
animals eat
This food tastes delicious.

foolish
silly
It is a foolish idea.

foot (feet)
the part of your body at the
end of your leg that you
stand and walk on
My father has very big feet.

football
a game played by two teams
who try to kick, run with, or
throw a ball across a goal line.
We play football every day.

forget (forgetting,
forgotten)
to not remember something
Don't forget your homework.

fork
▼ fork
1 something with
a handle and two
or more points that
is used for eating
*The fork goes to the
left of the plate.*
2 a tool used for digging.
Turn the soil with a fork.
3 the place where a road or
river divides in two
There is a fork in the road.

forward
toward the front
Take two steps forward.

fossil
the print of an animal or
plant that lived long ago
*Fossils show us what life was
like millions of years ago.*

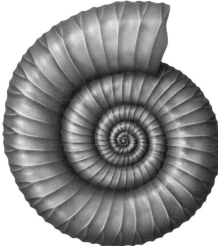

▲ fossil

fountain
a jet of water that is pushed
up into the air
*There is a fountain in the
center of the city.*

▲ fountain

▼ fox

fox (foxes)
a wild animal that looks like
a dog with a bushy tail
Baby foxes are called cubs.

fraction
a part of something
*A half, a third, and a quarter
are fractions.*

$$\frac{1}{4} = \text{a quarter}$$

▲ fraction

frame
the thing that fits around
a door, window, or picture
Frames can be wood or metal.

freckle
a small, reddish-brown spot
on a person's skin
Misha has freckles on her face.

free
1 not controlled
*Wednesday afternoon is free
time at our school.*
2 not costing anything
*I got a free pair of socks when
I bought these sneakers.*

freeze (freezing, froze, frozen)

to turn to ice because the temperature is very cold
Water freezes below 32°F.

▶ **frozen**

fresh

1 just picked, grown, or made
Fresh fruits and vegetables are good for you.
2 clean and pure
Go out and get some fresh air.

friend

a person you know and like
Good friends are very special.

▼ **friends**

friendly

easy to get along with
We have very friendly neighbors.

frighten (frightening, frightened)

to scare, to make afraid
Storms may frighten animals.

frog

an animal with long legs that lives on land and in water
There are frogs in the pond.

▲ **frog**

• Did you know? •

Almost any frog can jump 20 times its own length!

front

the part of something that is the most forward
I sit at the front of the class.

frost

white, icy powder that forms when it is very cold outside
The trees are covered with frost.

▲ **frost**

frown (frowning, frowned)

to have a sad, angry or worried look on your face
Try not to frown.

fruit

the part of a plant that has seeds, such as an apple, peach, or grape
There is fruit in this yogurt.

▶ **fruit**

fry (frying, fried)
to cook something using oil
Fry the fish until it is cooked.

▲ **fry**

full
containing as much as possible
Is the tank full yet?

fun
enjoyable
This Web site is really fun.

funny
making you laugh
The puppy is very funny.

▲ **funny**

fur (furry)
soft, thick hair on the skin of an animal
The kitten has soft, fluffy fur.

▼ **furry**

furniture
things in a room, such as chairs, tables, beds, and desks
We have new furniture in the dining room.

·Puzzle time·

How many pieces of furniture can you find in this word puzzle?

**bedtablechairdesk
bookshelfchestofdrawers**

answer
six

future
the time after now
In the future, we will have computers in our clothes.

fuzzy
1 not clear
These pictures are fuzzy.
2 soft and slightly hairy
The peach felt fuzzy.

chair

table

▼ **furniture**

bed

wardrobe

Gg

gallop (galloping, galloped)
how animals like horses or zebras run
See the zebras gallop away.

▲ galloping

game
an activity that has rules
Let's play a board game.

garage
1 a place to keep a car
The garage is next to the house.
2 a place where cars are repaired
The car is at the garage.

•Puzzle time•
See how many different words you can make from

garage

you should be able to make at least seven.

garden
land where flowers and plants can be grown
The garden is full of flowers.

▲ garden

gate
a door in a fence or wall
There is a gate between our garden and our neighbor's.

gentle
1 kind and careful not to hurt or disturb people or things
She is gentle with the animals.
2 not loud or strong
There is a gentle breeze blowing.

▼ gentle

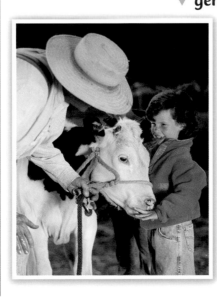

geography
the study of countries
I like geography because we read about people and places.

ghost
a dead person's spirit
Do you believe in ghosts?

▶ ghost

giant
an imaginary person who is very big
The story is about a giant.
see also fairy tale

▲ giant

gift
something given to someone; a present
Thank you for the lovely gift.

giraffe

a very tall wild animal
with a long neck
*Giraffes live
in Africa.*

◀ **giraffe**

girl

a female child
*There are 15
girls in our class.*

▶ **girl**

give (gave, given)

1 to let someone have
something
We gave our teacher a present.
2 to pass something to
someone
Give this cup to your sister.

glad

happy about something
We're so glad you could come.

glass

1 hard, clear material that is
used to make windows,
bottles, and mirrors
*The fish live in a
glass bowl.*
2 a container for
drinking from
*I have a glass of
water next to my
bed.*

▶ **glass**

•Puzzle time•

Which of these objects doesn't
belong?

a. glass   **b.** plate

c. jar

d. bottle

answer
b. plate

glasses

two pieces of glass or plastic
that you wear to protect your
eyes or to see better
I wear glasses for reading.

▼ **glasses**

gloomy

1 dark
It's a gloomy day.
2 sad
Don't look so gloomy, smile!

glove

a piece of clothing to wear on
your hands
Where are your gloves?

▲ **gloves**

glue (gluing, glued)

to stick things together
Glue the corners first.

goal

1 in a game like soccer or
hockey, the posts where the
player tries to put the ball
*The goalkeeper is a very
important player.*
2 the point given to a team
when it gets the ball inside
the goal
*That's another goal for our
team.*
3 something you hope to do
My goal is to be a teacher.

goat

an animal like a sheep, usually with horns
Goats will eat almost anything.

▲ **goat**

gold

1 a valuable, yellow metal
The ring is made of gold.
2 the color of this metal
The present is wrapped up in gold paper.

▼ **gold**

good (better, best)

1 of high quality
Our school is very good.
2 pleasant
I'm having a good time.
3 well-behaved
They are really good children.

good-bye (bye)

something you say when you are leaving someone
Good-bye and good luck!

goose (geese)

an animal like a big duck
There are geese on the farm.

▼ **geese**

goosebumps

little bumps on your skin that appear when you are cold or frightened
The ghost story gave me goosebumps.

gorilla

the biggest kind of ape
She studies gorillas.

▼ **gorilla**

• Did you know? •
Gorillas were relatively unknown until the mid-1800s. The first gorilla shown to the public was in a zoo in the United States, in 1911.

grandparents
(grandfather, grandmother)

the parents of your mother or father
Our grandparents live with us.

▲ **grandparents**

grape

a small, round, juicy fruit that grows in bunches
Grapes are red, green, or purple.

▶ **grapes**

grass

a green plant with thin leaves that grows over the ground
My brother is cutting the grass.

gravity

the force that pulls things toward Earth and other planets
Gravity is what makes things fall to the ground.

great

1 very good
This is a great song.
2 very large
We saw a great big bear.

greedy

wanting or taking more than
is necessary
*The story is about a greedy
king who loved gold.*

green

the color of leaves or grass
She wore a bright green hat.

ground

1 the surface of the Earth
that is under your feet
Lie on the ground and look up.
2 the soil on and under the
surface of the Earth
*We are digging a hole in the
ground near the pond.*

group

people or things that are
together or connected
*A group of us are playing in the
wading pool.*

grow (growing, grew, grown)

to become
larger or
longer
*The flowers
are growing
very well.*

▶ **grow**

guard (guarding, guarded)

to protect someone or
something
There is a guard outside.

▲ **guard**

guess (guessing, guessed)

to try to give the right answer
when you are not sure if it
is correct
Guess which hand it is in.

guinea pig

a furry animal with no tail
that people keep as a pet
*We have a guinea pig in our
classroom.*

▲ **guinea pig**

guitar

a stringed musical
instrument with a long
neck
*He plays the
guitar in
a band.*

◀ **guitar**

gun

a weapon that fires bullets
Guns are dangerous weapons.

gym

a place where people go to
exercise
*There are lots of different
machines at the gym.*

▲ **group**

Hh

hair
thin threads that grow on your skin and head
She has long brown hair.

half (halves)
one of two equal parts
Would you like half an apple?

ham
meat from a pig's leg
Some ham tastes salty.

hamburger
chopped beef cooked and served on a round bun
I can make hamburgers.

▶ **hamburger**

hammer
a tool used for hitting nails into wood
Use a hammer to bang the nail.

▼ **hammer**

hamster
a small, furry animal like a mouse.
Hamsters keep food in their cheeks.

▲ **hamster**

hand
the part of your body at the end of your arm
Your fingers and thumb are attached to your hand.

▲ **hand**

handle (handling, handled)
1 part of an object used for holding or carrying
He carried the pan by its handle.
2 to hold something and look at it carefully
Susan handled the kitten very gently.

hang (hanging, hanged, hung)
to attach the top part of something, leaving the lower part free or loose
Sam hung on to the branch.

▼ **hang**

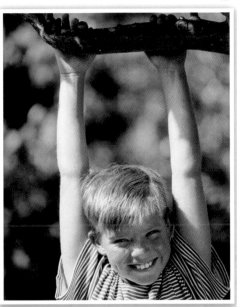

happen (happening, happened)
to be, to take place
Who knows what will happen?

happy
feeling pleased
We are happy today.

▲ **happy**

harbor

a safe place for ships and boats near land
The fishing boats leave the harbor early in the morning.

▲ harbor

hard

1 not soft
This bed is very hard.
2 difficult, not easy
The questions are very hard.

hat

a piece of clothing that you wear on your head
You must wear a hat in the sun.

▲ hat

hate (hating, hated)

to strongly dislike something or someone
My cat hates going to the vet.

head

1 the part of your body above your neck
Put your hands on your head.
2 a person who is the leader
My mother is the head of her company.

healthy

well and strong
Our new baby is a healthy girl.

hear (hearing, heard)

1 to get sounds using your ears
Can you hear the rain?
2 to get news or be told something
I hear you're moving away.

heart

1 the part of your body that pumps your blood
Your heart beats faster when you run.
2 the main part of something
It's in the heart of the city.
3 a shape that means love
Valentine cards are decorated with hearts.

see also shapes

· Did you know? ·

Your heart is made of special tissue called cardiac muscle, which never gets tired. This allows your heart to beat an amazing 30 million times every year!

large vein brings blood back to the heart

large artery sends blood to the body

artery takes blood from the heart back to the lungs

veins bring blood back to the heart from the lungs

atrium (upper chamber)

ventricle (lower chamber)

▲ heart

heat (heating, heated)
to make something warm
Heat the soup, but don't boil it.

heavy
weighing a lot
These books are really heavy.

·Puzzle time·
Can you match the opposites
in A and B?

A	B
heavy	old
sad	rich
young	light
poor	happy

answers
heavy/light sad/happy
young/old poor/rich

hedgerow
a row of bushes
*Many birds and small animals
live in hedgerows.*

heel
1 the back part of
your foot
*Your heel is under
your ankle.*
2 The part of a
shoe that is under
your heel.
*Mom's shoes have
high heels.*

heel

▲ heel

height
how tall something is
*What is your height in feet and
inches?*

helicopter
an aircraft with blades on top
that spin and make it fly
*Helicopters can land in smaller
spaces than planes.*

▼ helicopter

hello
what you say when you see
or meet someone, or when
you answer the telephone
Hello! How are you?

helmet
a hat that protects your head
*Always wear a helmet when you
ride your bike.*

▲ helmet

help (helping, helped)
to make it easier for someone
to do something
Let me help you lift that.

hen
a female chicken
Hens lay eggs.

here
in this place
I like it here.

hibernate (hibernating, hibernated)
to sleep during cold weather
*Some animals hibernate
in the winter.*

· Did you know? ·
Some animals hibernate
because there is less food
available to them during the
winter. A hibernating animal
needs very little energy to stay
alive, and is able to live off fat
in its body until the weather
warms up again.

hide (hiding, hid, hidden)
to put yourself or something
out of sight
Hide the presents, she's coming.

high

1 a long way from the bottom to the top
Mount Everest is the highest mountain on Earth.
2 a long way above
The plane is high above us.

▼ high

• Did you know? •
Mount Everest is the highest point on Earth at 29,031 feet (8,848 meters), that's 27 times higher than the Eiffel Tower in Paris, France!

hill

ground that is raised
Run down the hill.

▼ hills

hippopotamus
(hippopotamuses, hippopotami)

a large animal that lives near rivers and lakes in Africa
Hippopotamuses leave the water at night to eat grass.

▲ hippopotamuses

history

things that have happened in the past
Our town's history is very interesting.

hit (hitting, hit)

to swing your hand or something you are holding against something else
Hit the ball as hard as you can.

▶ hit

hobby (hobbies)

something that you enjoy doing in your spare time
My hobbies are skateboarding and listening to music.

▲ hobby

hockey

a team game played on ice, where skaters use sticks to try to hit a rubber disk into a goal area
Hockey is a very fast game.

hold (holding, held)

to have something in your hands or arms
Would you like to hold the baby?

hole

an opening or an empty space
There is a hole in the bottom of the bag.

holiday

a special day
It is a very special holiday.

hollow
empty inside
The log is hollow.

hologram
a picture made with a laser
There is a hologram on the sticker.

home
the place where you live
What time will you get home?

homework
schoolwork you do at home
I do my homework when I get home from school.

honey
a sweet, sticky food made by bees
Put honey in your yogurt.

hood
a piece of clothing that covers your head, usually attached to a coat or jacket
Put your hood up, it's raining.

▶ **hood**

hoof (hooves)
the foot of an animal, such as a deer, horse, or goat
Horses have very thick hooves.

hook
a piece of metal or plastic for hanging up or catching things
Hang your jacket on the hook.

hoop
a large ring of metal, wood, or plastic
It's fun to play with hoops.

▼ **hoops**

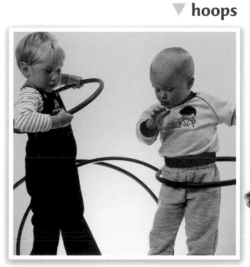

hop (hopping, hopped)
1 to jump on one foot, or make a small jump with two feet
Can you hop on one foot?

hope (hoping, hoped)
to wish for something
I hope you have a good time.

horn
1 one of the hard, pointed things on an animal's head
Goats and cows have horns.
2 something that you push or blow into to make a sound
The horn is very loud.

▼ **horn**

horrible
bad or unpleasant
What a horrible color.

horse
a large animal with four legs, a mane, and a tail
My brother can ride a horse.

▲ **horse**

hospital
the place where sick or injured people go to get better
Have you ever had to stay in the hospital?

hot
at a very high temperature
Mercury is the hottest planet because it is closest to the sun.

hotdog
a sausage in a long bun
Would you like a hotdog?

hotel
a place people pay to stay at
There's a hotel on the beach.

hour
sixty minutes
The film is an hour long.

house
a building that people live in
My friend lives in the house across the street.

human (human being)
a person, not an animal
Humans are very intelligent.

hump
a large bump
The camel has a large hump on its back.

hungry
feeling that you need food
I'm hungry. What's for dinner?

hunt (hunting, hunted)
1 to look for something or someone
We hunted everywhere for the other shoe.
2 to try to catch wild animals
The owl hunted for mice at night.

hurricane
a very strong wind storm
Hurricanes can cause lots of damage.

▲ **hurricane**

hurry (hurrying, hurried)
to do something quickly
Hurry and get your coat.

hurt (hurting, hurt)
1 to cause pain or harm
The dentist won't hurt you.
2 to feel pain
My knee hurts.

husband
the man a woman is married to
Dad is Mom's husband.

▲ **hunt**

•Puzzle time•
Can you match A with B?

A	B
dishwasher	bedroom
bed	bathroom
shower	kitchen

answers
dishwasher/kitchen
wardrobe/bedroom
shower/bathroom

• Did you know? •
Owls have sharp claws called talons, which they use to grab their prey.

huge
very big
There was a huge dog in the yard.

Ii

ice
water that is so cold that it
has frozen and become hard
Do you want ice in your water?

▲ ice

iceberg
a large piece of ice that floats
in the ocean
*Most of an iceberg is hidden
under water.*

▲ iceberg

ice cream
a frozen, sweet
food that is
usually made of
milk or cream
*Ice cream tastes
good on hot days.*

▲ ice cream

ice skate (ice skating, ice skated)
to move across ice
wearing boots with
a metal blade on
the bottom
*We're learning how to
ice skate.*

► ice skating

icing
a sweet covering for cakes,
also called frosting
Spread the icing on the cake.

▼ icing

idea
a plan or a thought about
how to do something
*Do you have any ideas about
how we can raise money for the
school trip?*

igloo
an Inuit house
made of
blocks of
snow and ice
*The Inuits only
live in igloos in
the winter.*

▲ igloo

ill
not well, sick
*I'm sorry to hear that
you're ill.*

imaginary
not real
*The story is about an
imaginary cat with
special powers.*

imitate (imitating, imitated)
to copy
*He can imitate the way our
teacher talks.*

immediately
now; at once; right away
*Please put your clothes away
immediately.*

important
1 serious, useful, or valuable
It is a very important discovery.
2 powerful
*The mayor is an important
person in our town.*

impossible

not able to be, be done, or to happen
That's impossible—you can't be in two places at once!

information

facts or knowledge about someone or something
There is a lot of information about our school on our Web site.

initial

the first letter of a person's name
What is your middle initial?

injection

a way of putting medicine into your body using a special needle
The nurse comes to our school to give injections.

injure (injuring, injured)

to hurt or harm yourself or someone else
Luckily, no one was injured in the crash.

ink

colored liquid that is used for writing, drawing, or printing
Sign your name in ink.

◄ **ink**

insect

a small animal with six legs, wings, and a body that has three parts
Beetles, butterflies, and bees are all kinds of insects.

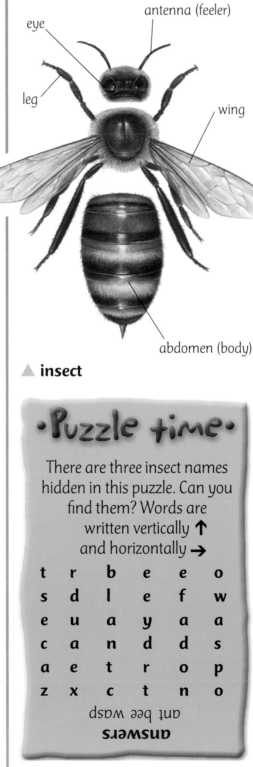

eye
antenna (feeler)
leg
wing
abdomen (body)

▲ **insect**

•Puzzle time•

There are three insect names hidden in this puzzle. Can you find them? Words are written vertically ↑ and horizontally →

t	r	b	e	e	o
s	d	l	e	f	w
e	u	a	y	a	a
c	a	n	d	d	s
a	e	t	r	o	p
z	x	c	t	n	o

answers
ant bee wasp

inside

in or into a place or container
Stay inside until it stops raining.

instrument

something people use to do a job
We use instruments to make music.

triangle
tambourine
drum
guitar

▲ **instruments**

interested

wanting to pay attention to something or someone so that you can learn more
Sam is interested in sports.

interesting

exciting in a way that keeps your attention
E-mailing children in other countries is really interesting.

Internet

a huge system of linked computers all over the world that lets people communicate with each other
We use the Internet at home and at school.

interrupt (interrupting, interrupted)

to break in or stop someone who is doing something or saying something
The phone call interrupted our conversation.

invade (invading, invaded)

to attack or go into a place in large numbers
The Vikings left their ships and invaded the country.

▼ **invade**

invent (inventing, invented)

to make something that has not been made before
Computers were invented about 65 years ago.

invention

something new that someone makes, or produces, for the first time
The telephone is the invention of Alexander Graham Bell.

car (1885)

telephone (1876)

lightbulb (1879)

flying machine (1874)

tape recording (1899)

▲ **inventions**

invisible

not possible to see
You can't read it, it is written in invisible ink!

invite (inviting, invited)

to ask someone if they would like to do something, such as come to a party
Ellie always invites lots of people to her parties.

invitation

a note or a card that asks you to go to a party
Did you get an invitation to Ellie's party?

iron

1 a strong, hard metal
The machinery is made of iron

▼ **iron**

2 a machine for smoothing clothes
Be careful, the iron gets very hot.

island

a piece of land that has water all around it
There are thousands of islands in the Pacific Ocean.

▲ **island**

Jj

jacket
a piece of clothing
like a short coat
*You should take
a jacket with you.*

▶ **jacket**

jail
a prison;
a place where
people are kept by the police
*The thief was put in jail for
seven months.*

jam
a sweet food made from fruit
*We sometimes have bread and
jam for our snack.*

jar
a glass container for
storing food
*Jam and honey are
sold in jars.*

▲ **jar**

jealous
feeling angry or bad because
you want something that
someone else has
He is jealous of our grades.

jeans
pants made of
denim
*My favorite
clothes are
jeans and
a t-shirt.*

▼ **jeans**

jeep
an open vehicle that is used
for driving over rough
ground
Drive the jeep across the field.

jellyfish
a sea animal that floats on
the surface and can sting
*There are many different types
of jellyfish.*

▶ **jellyfish**

jet
a fast airplane
*There are several jet fighters in
the air show.*

▲ **jets**

jewelry
things such as necklaces,
bracelets, and earrings that
you wear for decoration
She wore jewelry to the party.

▼ **jewelry**

earrings

bracelet

necklace

jigsaw puzzle
a puzzle made from shaped
pieces that you fit together to
make a picture
The jigsaw puzzle has 40 pieces.

▲ **jigsaw puzzle**

job
work that you get paid for
doing
She has a new job.

join (joining, joined)
1 become a member of a club
or other group
*Lots of people join the Cubs,
Scouts, and Brownies every year.*
2 to stick or fasten together
Join the two pieces of cardboard.

joke
a funny story that is told to make people laugh
Do you know any good jokes?

jolly
happy
He's a jolly person.

journey
a trip
We were very tired after the long journey.

judo
a Japanese fighting sport
In judo, people try to throw each other to the floor.

juggle (juggling, juggled)
to keep a set of balls or other objects in the air by throwing them up and catching them again, one after the other
I like watching the clowns juggling at the circus.

juice
liquid from fruit or vegetables
Would you like some juice?

▼ juice

jump (jumping, jumped)
to push yourself off the ground with both feet
Jump as high as you can.

▲ jump

jump rope
a long piece of rope that is used for skipping
We took turns playing with the jump rope.

jungle
a thick forest in a hot country
The trees and plants in a jungle grow very close together.

▼ jungle
canopy
middle branches
forest floor

• Did you know? •
There are more kinds of animals and plants living in jungles than any other areas of the world.

just
to have happened a very short time ago
I've just come home from work.

Kk

kaleidoscope

a tube with pictures or pieces of colored glass or plastic at one end that you look through and turn to see changing patterns
The kaleidoscope was invented in 1816.

pattern

tube can be turned to make patterns

▼ **kaleidoscope**

colored glass

kangaroo

an Australian animal that keeps its young in a pouch on the front of its body
Kangaroos have big, strong back legs.

▲ **kangaroos**

karate

a Japanese fighting sport
In karate, you fight using your hands and feet.

◄ **karate**

keep (keeping, kept)

1 to continue to have something
You can keep the library books for two weeks.
2 to continue to do something
Don't keep staring at that man.
3 to have something in a certain place
The paints and crayons are kept on the shelf.

kettle

a container or machine for boiling water
I'll put the kettle on and make some tea.

key

1 a special piece of metal used to open a lock
Turn the key to the right.
2 one of the parts of a computer or piano that you press with your fingers
Type the file name and then press the "enter" key.
3 a set of answers or an explanation of symbols
There is a key at the back of the book.

◄ **key**

keyboard

the set of keys on a computer or a piano that you press to type or make a sound
This is a special keyboard with letters and pictures.

▲ **keyboard**

kick (kicking, kicked)

to swing your foot at something
Kick it into the net!

▲ **kick**

kill (killing, killed)

to cause someone or something to die
Some weeds kill other plants.

kind

helpful, pleasant, and thoughtful
It's very kind of you to think of me.

king

a royal man who rules a country
Do you think the prince will become king?

▶ **king**

kiss (kissing, kissed)

to touch someone else with your lips
Mom kissed us all good night.

kitchen

the room in a house for preparing food
There are good smells coming from the kitchen.

kite

a toy made of light wood and cloth, paper, or plastic that you fly at the end of a long string
I like to fly my kite on windy days.

▲ **kite**

kitten

a baby cat
Our cat has two kittens.

▲ **kittens**

knee

the part of your leg that bends
If you lift something heavy, you should bend your knees.

knife (knives)

a tool with a blade for cutting things into pieces
Put the knife to the right of your plate.

▲ **knife**

knit (knitting, knitted)

to join wool together with long metal sticks
Jodie can knit.

▼ **knitting**

knock (knocking, knocked)

to hit something to make a noise
Knock on the back door.

knot

the place where two pieces of string or rope are tied together
There are many different ways to tie knots.

▲ **knot**

L l

label
a piece of paper or cloth that gives information about the thing it is attached to
Always put a label on your floppy disks.

lace
fine cloth made with patterns of tiny holes
The doll's dress is made of long, white lace.

▲ lace

ladder
a piece of equipment made from two long bars joined together by short bars, used for climbing up to reach high places
Dad uses a ladder when he paints the house.

ladybug
a round insect that is red with black spots
Ladybugs are good for the garden.

▲ ladybug

lake
a big area of water that has land all around it
The lake was surrounded by forests and mountains.

▲ lake

lamb
a young sheep, or the meat from that animal
Lambs are born in the spring.

▲ lamb

lamp
a machine that gives light
Switch on the lamp, it's too dark to see.

◄ lamp

land
1 ground
We bought a plot of land.
2 the dry part of the Earth
The sailors were very happy to see land.
3 a place or a country
It is in a magical land far away.

land (landing, landed)
to reach the ground after being in the air
The plane lands at 2:45 P.M.

language
words used by people to communicate with each other
Our teacher speaks two languages, English and Chinese.

lap
1 the top of your legs when you are sitting down
My cat likes to sit on my lap when I'm reading.
2 once around a track
They ran 12 laps of the track.

large
big
We ate a large piece of cake.

laser
a powerful light, or the machine that makes it
We saw a terrific laser show at the museum.

a b c d e f g h i j k l m

last

1 after the others
We finished last in the sack race.
2 the one that happened the shortest time ago
We went to Italy for our last vacation.

last (lasting, lasted)

to continue to work or to be
How long will the batteries last?

late

1 after the usual or correct time
Sorry I'm late!
2 toward the end of a period of time
It was late on Sunday afternoon.

laugh (laughing, laughed)

to make a sound that shows you are happy or that you think something is funny
We laughed at Dad's silly joke.

▲ **laughing**

law

a rule made by the government
A new law has been passed.

lawn

a place in a garden or a park that is covered with grass that is cut short
Mow the lawn.

lay (laying, laid)

1 to put in a place
Lay the coats over the back of the chair.
2 to make an egg
The hens lay eggs most days.

lazy

1 a name given to someone who doesn't like work
She's the laziest girl in the class.
2 not busy, relaxed
We had a nice, lazy weekend.

lead (leading, led)

1 to show someone the way
The dog led them to the children.
2 to be in the front
The champion is leading the parade.

lean (leaning, leaned)

1 to be in or move into a position that is not straight
Lean over the fence and pick up the ball.
2 to rest against something
Chris was leaning against the wall, watching the game.

leap (leaping, leapt)

to jump into the air or over something
The frog leaped into the pond.

▼ **leap**

learn (learning, learned)

to get knowledge or information about a subject
We are learning to paint pictures at school.

▲ **learn**

leave (leaving, left)

1 to go away from a place
What time are you leaving?
2 to put a thing in a place or to let a thing stay in a place
You can leave your bike in the yard.

leg

1 the part of your body that you stand up with, between your hip and your foot
Dad's legs are a lot longer than mine.
2 the part of a table or chair that holds it up
One of the chair legs is broken.

lemon

a sour, yellow fruit
We squeezed some lemons to make lemonade.

▲ **lemon**

lend (lending, lent)

to let someone have or use something that they will return after using
Lend me a pen, please.
see also borrow

leopard

a large cat with yellow or white fur and black spots
Leopards are beautiful animals.

▲ **leopard**

leotard

a stretchy piece of clothing that you wear for dancing or exercising
We wear leotards in ballet class.

lesson

a time in which someone is taught something such as a skill or a subject
I take piano lessons every Thursday after school.

let (letting, let)

1 to allow someone to do something
Will your mom let you sleep over tonight?
2 to allow something to happen
Just let the ball fall.

letter

1 one of the signs of the alphabet used in writing
There are five letters in James' name.
2 a written message that you put in an envelope and send or give someone
Can you send either a letter or an e-mail?

·Puzzle time·

The words in this letter are backwards—what does the letter say?

raeD amdnarG,
I ma ta emoh yadot. I evah a dloc. I epoh uoy era llew.
,evoL
kraM

answer
Dear Grandma, I am at home today. I have a cold. I hope you are well. Love, Mark

lettuce

a green, leafy vegetable eaten in salads
We're growing lettuce this year.

▲ **lettuce**

library

a place where books are kept
I borrowed this book from the school library.

lick (licking, licked)
to put your tongue on something
Lick your ice cream, it's going to drip.

lie (lying, lay, lain)
to have your body flat on the floor, ground, or bed.
We put our towels on the sand and lay down.

lie (lying, lied)
to say something that is not the truth
They lied about their age.

life (lives)
1 the time between when you are born and when you die
He had a long, happy life.
2 being alive
Do you think there is life on other planets?

lifeboat
a boat that helps people who are in danger at sea
The fishermen were rescued by the lifeboat just in time.

▼ lifeboat

lift (lifting, lifted)
to move something to a higher place
It took two people to lift our piano.

lift
when someone gives you a ride in their car, and takes you somewhere you want to go.
My neighbor gives me a lift to school every day.

light
1 energy or brightness from the sun or a lamp that lets you see things
Is there enough light to take a picture?
2 a machine that makes light
Turn off the light, it's time for bed.

◄ light

white light

glass triangle (prism)

lighthouse
a tower on the coast that has a bright light that flashes to warn ships
There's a lighthouse at the end of the beach.

lightning
electrical light in the sky during a storm.
We could see lightning in the distance.

▲ lightning

like (liking, liked)
1 to enjoy something or be fond of someone or something
I really like skateboarding.
2 to want
What would you like for your birthday?

light splits into the seven colors of the rainbow as it passes through the prism

line

1 a long, thin mark
Draw a line through the mistakes.
2 a piece of string, rope, or wire
Hang the clothes on the line.
3 a row
There is a line of trees along the path in the park.

lion

a large wild cat
Lions live in Africa.

▼ lion

lips

the edges of your mouth
The cat came in, licking his lips.

liquid

something, such as water, that is not hard and can be poured
There's some liquid soap in the bathroom.

listen (listening, listened)

to pay attention to sound
Sorry, what did you say? I wasn't listening.

litter

1 bits of trash lying on the ground
We picked up all the litter in the playground.
2 the group of babies that an animal has at one time
Our dog had a litter of puppies last night.

little

small, not large or not much
We gave the cat a little milk.

live (living, lived)

1 to be alive
My great-grandfather lived to be 80 years old.
2 to have your home in a certain place
They live in France now.

•Puzzle time•

Can you fill in the missing letters to find out what is in the living room?

a. s _ _ a

b. t_l_v_si_n

c. b _ _ k she_f

d. a_mch _ ir

e. la _ p

answers
a. sofa b. television c. bookshelf
d. armchair e. lamp

living room

a room in a house for sitting and relaxing in
The TV is in the living room.

lizard

a short, four-legged animal that lays eggs
A lizard's blood changes temperature to match the temperature around it.

▲ lizard

loaf (loaves)

something, such as bread, that is baked in one piece
Get a loaf of bread and some milk from the store.

lobster

a sea animal with eight legs and two claws
We saw a lobster through the glass bottom of the boat.

▲ lobster

lock

an object that is used to close something, usually opened and shut with a key
There's a lock on the chest.

lock (locking, locked)
to close or fasten something with a key
Have you locked the door?

locker
a small cupboard that can be locked, where you can put your belongings
I've left my book in my locker.

log
a thick piece of a tree
It's cold in here—put another log on the fire.

▲ logs

lonely
feeling sad that you are by yourself
Come over if you get lonely.

long
1 measuring a big distance from one end to the other
Is it a long walk?
2 continuing for a large amount of time
It's a very long movie.

look (looking, looked)
to pay attention to something that you see
Look at that hot-air balloon.

loose
1 not tight
Wear loose clothes.
2 free to move
The lions were set loose.

lose (losing, lost)
1 to not be able to find something
He keeps losing his glasses.
2 to not win a competition or a game
Our team lost the race.

loud
not quiet; making a lot of noise
Turn it down, that's too loud!

love (loving, loved)
to like someone or something very much
We love our new baby.

lovely
very beautiful or pleasant
It's a lovely day.

low
close to the ground, not high
There are some low clouds around the hills.

lucky
1 fortunate, having good things happen to you
They're lucky they won.
2 giving good luck
These are my lucky soccer cleats.

lunch
a meal that you eat in the middle of the day
Why don't we meet for lunch?

▼ lunch

lungs
parts of your body inside your chest that help you breathe
You have two lungs protected by bones called ribs.

▼ lungs

windpipe
lung
tube

Mm

machine

a piece of equipment that is used to do a job
Washing machines wash, rinse, and spin your clothes.

▲ machine

magic

a power to make strange things happen
I can do magic tricks.

magnet

a piece of metal that makes some other metal objects move toward it
Use a magnet to pick up all the pins.

▲ magnet

main

the most important or the biggest
We'll meet you in front of the main entrance.

make (making, made)

1 to create or build something
The computer was made in a factory.
2 to cause something to happen or be a certain way
That joke always makes me laugh.

male

a man or boy, or an animal that cannot produce eggs or have babies
Male elephants are bigger than female elephants.

mammal

the group of animals that give birth to live babies and make milk for them to drink
The blue whale is the largest mammal.

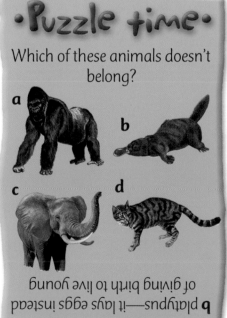

•Puzzle time•

Which of these animals doesn't belong?

a

b

c

d

answer
b platypus—it lays eggs instead of giving birth to live young

man (men)

an adult male
My father is a tall man.

many

large in number
There are many good reasons to use the Internet.

map

a drawing that shows where things are in a building, city, country, or other place
We studied a map of the world.

▲ map

marble

1 a type of hard stone
The walls are made of marble.
2 a small glass or metal ball used to play a game
I won two marbles in that last game.

▼ marbles

march (marching, marched)

to walk with regular steps
The band marched at the front of the parade.

margin

the long, blank space that runs down the edge of a page
Please write your comments in the margin.

mark

1 a sign or shape
Put a mark to show where your house is.
2 a spot or a dark patch on something that makes it look bad
There is a mark on the carpet.

market

a place where you can buy food, clothes, plants and other things
Some markets are outdoors.

▲ market

marmalade

jam that is made from oranges
We had toast and marmalade with our breakfast.

marry (marrying, married)

to become husband and wife
He got married three years ago.

◀ married

mask

something that you put over your face to hide or protect it
He always wore a mask.

▶ mask

mat

a piece of material that covers a floor or table
Wipe your feet on the mat.

match (matches)

1 a small stick that makes a flame when you rub it against something
We have special long matches for lighting the fire.
2 a contest or game
That's the best tennis match I've ever seen.

▼ matches

mathematics (math)

the study of numbers or shapes
Mathematics is studied in schools.

•Puzzle time•

Use the code to find the answer to this math problem

A	B	C	D	E	F	G	H	I	J
1	2	3	4	5	6	7	8	9	10

K	L	M	N	O	P	Q	R
11	12	13	14	15	16	17	18

S	T	U	V	W	X	Y	Z
19	20	21	22	23	24	25	26

N + F = T

answer
14 + 6 = 20

meadow

a field with grass and flowers
The meadow was covered in pretty flowers.

▼ meadow

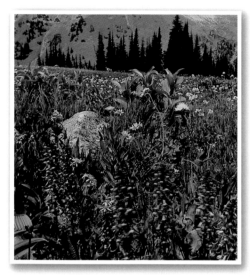

meal

a time when food is eaten, or the food itself
We had a huge meal last night.

mean

cruel or unkind
Don't be mean to each other.

meaning

the information that is supposed to be understood from words and signs
What's the meaning of this?

measles

an illness that gives you a high temperature and lots of red spots
My brother has the measles.

measure (measures, measuring, measured)

to find out the size or amount of something
Measure each side of the room.

measure

an action taken to make sure that something happens
We must take measures to make sure the competition goes ahead as planned.

meat

food made from animals
People who don't eat meat are called vegetarians.

mechanic

a person who fixes cars and machines
He's a good mechanic.

medal

a piece of metal that is given as a prize for winning a competition or for doing something special
He won a medal for bravery.

▶ medal

medicine

1 something that you take when you are not well so that you will get better
You have to take this medicine three times a day.
2 the study of illness and injury
She is studying medicine.

medium

a middle size between large and small
I'd like a medium popcorn, please.

meet (meeting, met)

1 to know someone for the first time
We met the first day of school.
2 to go to the same place as another person
Meet me at the corner.

melody (melodies)

a song, or the tune of a song
The song has a strange but beautiful melody.

melon

a fruit with a hard skin and flat seeds
Melons can be green, yellow, or orange.

▶ melon

melt (melting, melted)
to change from a solid to a liquid when heated
The ice melted in the heat.

▶ **melt**

memory (memories)
1 something that you remember from the past
Photographs bring back memories.
2 the ability to remember things
Do you have a good memory?
3 the part of a computer where information is stored
This computer has more memory than our old one.
see also remember and remind

mend (mending, mended)
to repair
Could you help me mend the tire?

▲ **mend**

menu
1 the list of food in a café or restaurant
The waiter brought us each a menu.
2 a list of things seen on a computer screen
Click here to go back to the main menu.

messy
not tidy
This room is very messy.

message
information for a person from someone else
Leave a message for him on the notepad.

metal
hard material, such as gold, silver, copper, or iron
Silver is a precious metal.

▲ **metal**

microphone
something that is used for recording sounds or making them louder
Speak into the microphone.

▶ **microphone**

microscope
something that makes small things look much bigger
We looked at a hair under the microscope.

▶ **microscope**

microwave
an oven that cooks food very quickly using waves of electricity, not heat
Put the soup in the microwave for six minutes.

▲ **microwave**

middle
the center or the part of something that is between the beginning and the end
We sat down in the middle of the row.

midnight
12:00 in the middle of the night
We stay up until midnight on New Year's Eve.

migrate (migrating, migrated)
when animals travel to another country or area in search of food or to reproduce
Some birds migrate to Africa.

mild
1 not too strong or serious
She had a mild case of flu.
2 not tasting too strong or too spicy
It's a mild chili.
3 not too cold
The weather is mild today.

▶ **milk**

milk
white liquid that female humans and other mammals produce to feed their babies
We drink cow's and goat's milk.

minus (minuses)
the sign used in math when taking one number away from another
Twenty-five minus five equals twenty. ▼ **minus**

25 − 5 = 20

minute
sixty seconds
We waited for 20 minutes, but they didn't come.

mirror
special glass that you can see your reflection or what's behind you in
Go look in the mirror—you look really funny.

▶ **mirror**

miserable
very unhappy
Don't look so miserable.

miss
not to hit a target
He missed the basket.

mistake
something that is wrong
We all make mistakes.

mittens
gloves that do not have separate places for each finger
Dress warmly and wear your mittens.

◀ **mittens**

mix (mixing, mixed)
to put different things together
Mix all the ingredients together in a bowl.

moan (moaning, moaned)
to complain about something
Sam moaned about all the homework he had to do.

model
1 a small copy of something, such as a plane or a building
We made a model plane over the weekend.
▶ **model**
2 a person whose job is to show clothes
She wants to be a model when she's older.
3 a particular type of something
This computer is the most up-to-date model.

money

coins and paper that you use
to buy things with
*Have you spent all your money
already?*

▲ **money**

monitor

the part of a computer that
shows the screen
*It's easier to see on a big
monitor.*

monkey

an animal with a long tail
that uses its legs to climb
*We watched the monkeys at
the zoo.*

▼ **monkey**

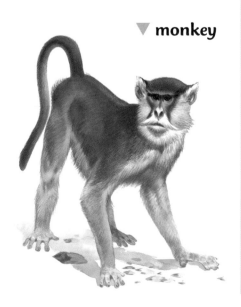

monster

a frightening creature in
stories and films
*The monster
chased them
into the
forest.*

◀ **monster**

month

one of the 12 parts of
the year
*Most months are 30 or 31
days long, except February.*

moon

the small object, like a planet,
that travels around
the Earth
*The moon
is full
tonight.*

▶ **moon**

more (most)

1 stronger or greater than
*This book is more interesting
than the last one I read.*
2 a larger or an additional
amount or number
Is there any more cake?

morning

the part of the day between
the time the sun comes up
and noon
*We get up at the same time
every morning.*

mosque

a building where Muslim
people go to pray
*The mosque is in the center of
the town.*

▲ **mosque**

moth

an insect that is similar to
a butterfly
*Moths are more active
at night.*

▶ **moth**

mother

a woman who has a child, or a female animal that has young
My mother is a nurse.

motor

the part of a machine that uses power to make it work
There is a motor in the washing machine.

motorcycle (motorbike)

a vehicle with two wheels and a seat for people to ride on
Dad has a new motorcycle.

▲ **motorcycle**

mountain

land that has been pushed up very high
Some mountains have snow on top all year round.

▲ **mountain**

mouse (mice)

1 a small animal with a long tail and a pointed nose
There are mice in the field.
2 the part of a computer with a ball in it that you move by hand to move things around on the screen
You can play this game using a mouse.

▲ **mouse**

•Puzzle time•

Can you spot five differences between these two pictures?

answers
1 flag 2 scarf 3 mustache 4 smoke 5 moon

mouth

the part of your face that you use to talk and eat
Don't talk with your mouth full.

move (moving, moved)

to change the position of something
Could you move, please? I can't see the TV.

movie

a story that is told using pictures that move; a film
Would you like to see a movie?

mow (mowing, mowed)

to cut grass using a special machine
Dad mows the grass every week.

much

a lot
Thank you very much for inviting me.

mud

wet soil or earth
The football players were covered with mud.

▲ **mud**

mug

a cup with tall sides
*Do you want a mug of hot
chocolate?*

▲ **mug**

multiply (multiplying, multiplied)

to add a number to itself,
often more than once
four multiplied by two is eight.

▼ **multiply**

$$4 \times 2 = 8$$
$$3 \times 3 = 9$$
$$3 \times 4 = 12$$
$$7 \times 2 = 14$$

mumps

an illness that makes your
neck swell
Have you had the mumps?

munch (munching, munched)

to eat something noisily
*The rabbit munched on carrots
and lettuce.*

muscle

one of the parts of the body
that tightens and relaxes to
cause movement
Relax your muscles.

▼ **muscles**

shoulder
muscle

arm muscle

thigh
muscle

calf
muscle

• **Did you know?** •
The human body has about 620
muscles that are used thousands
of times every day. For instance,
you use about 200 muscles every
time you take a single step, and
the tiny muscles that move your
eyes are used up to 100,000
times a day!

museum

a place where old, important,
valuable, or interesting things
are kept so that people can go
and look at them
*There is a toy museum,
a science museum, and an
art museum.*

mushroom

a small vegetable that has
a stem with a round top
*Do you want mushrooms on
your pizza?*

▼ **mushrooms**

music

a pattern of sounds that is
sung or played on special
instruments
*Can you read
music?*

▲ **music**

must

to have to do something
*You must lock the door before
you go to bed at night.*

mysterious

something strange, secret, or
difficult to understand
*He is a mysterious person—we
don't know much about him.*

Nn

nail
1 a thin, sharp piece of metal with one flat end that you hit with a hammer
Hang the picture on that nail.
2 the hard covering on the ends of your fingers and toes
He bites his nails.

▲ nails

name
what a person or object is called
What's your name?

narrow
having only a short distance from one side to the other
The road is very narrow.

▲ narrow

nasty
very unpleasant or bad
That's a nasty cut.

nation
a country and the people who live there
It is a poor nation.

naughty
badly behaved
My little sister can be very naughty.

•Puzzle time•

Someone has been naughty, and written this message backwards. Can you work out what it says?

ouy dlouhs od ruoy krowemoh yreve yad.

answer
you should do your homework every day.

navy
the ships and people that fight for a country at sea during a war
My cousin is in the navy.

near
close by, not far
There's a bus stop near the zoo.

neat
1 clean or organized
His room is always neat.
2 clearly presented
You have very neat handwriting.

neck
the part of your body that attaches your head to your shoulders
Put a scarf around your neck.

necklace
a piece of jewelry that you wear around your neck
That's a beautiful necklace.

▲ necklace

needle
1 a thin, sharp piece of metal with a hole through it, used for sewing
First, thread the needle.
2 a thin, sharp piece of metal through which injections are given
The needle will not hurt you.

▲ needle

a b c d e f g h i j k l m

neighbor

a person who lives near
another person
*We invited all our friends and
neighbors to the party.*

nephew

the son of your sister or
brother
*My nephew is staying with us
for a few days.*
see also at family

nervous

worried or frightened, not
able to relax
*She's a little nervous about
being in the school play.*

nest

a place birds make to lay
their eggs
*There's a robin's nest in
that tree.*

▼ **nest**

• Did you know? •
The weaverbird's nest is a work of
art. Using its beak, it weaves straw
and grass into a large nest with its
own roof and entrance!

net

material that is made by
joining pieces of string or
thread together, leaving
spaces between them
*We use a small net when we
go fishing.*

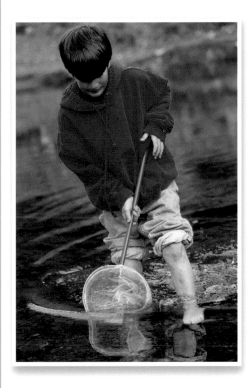

▲ **net**

network

a system of things or people
that are connected.
*There's a computer network
at school.*

never

not at any time, not ever
I've never been to China.

new

not old or used
Is that a new jacket?

news

information about something
that is happening now or that
happened a short time ago
*Write soon and send us all
your news.*

newspaper

sheets of paper that are
printed with words and
pictures to tell you what is
happening in the world.
*Have you read today's
newspaper?*

▲ **newspapers**

next

the one that is nearest
or immediately after
another one
Who's next on the list?

nice

enjoyable, good, pleasant
Did you have a nice time?

niece

the daughter of your sister
or brother
Her niece works in a bank.

night

the time of day between when the sun sets and rises again
The moon can be seen at night.

▼ night

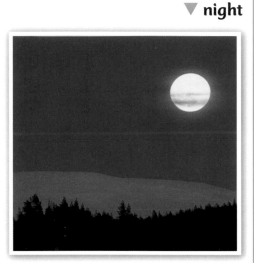

nightgown

a dress to sleep in
Put on your nightgown and get into bed.

nightmare

a bad dream
Nightmares can be very scary.

nobody

no one, no person
There's nobody home.

nod (nodding, nodded)

to quickly move your head up and down
She nodded her head in reply.

noise

loud sounds
Keep the noise down, will you?

none

not any, not one
Sorry, there is none left in the box.

nonsense

something that does not make any sense or mean anything
The television show was complete nonsense.

noodles

very thin strips of food that are usually made from flour, water, and eggs, then boiled
Do you want rice or noodles?

▲ noodles

no one

nobody, not one person
I have no one to talk to.

normal (normally)

not out of the ordinary
We normally go to bed late.

nose

the part of your face that you use for breathing and smelling things
Breathe in deeply through your nose.

• Did you know? •

When we smell something, scent particles go into our nose, which sends messages to our brain. If something makes us sneeze, the rush of air out of the nose can reach 100 miles (160 km) per hour!

▼ nose

olfactory (smelling) nerve

mucous lining

scent-sensitive cell

nose

note

1 a very short written message
Mother wrote a note to the school.
2 a musical sound, or the mark to show a musical sound
The opera singer can hit very high notes.

▲ note

nothing

not any thing; zero
There's nothing in the box, it's empty.

notice (noticing, noticed)

1 to see something or be aware that it is there
Did you notice if anyone was there?
2 a written message that tells people something
We got a notice saying school would be closed.

now

this time; the present
Where are you going now?

number

1 a word or symbol that means the amount, quantity, or order of something
Some people think seven is a lucky number.
2 the numbers you press on a phone to call someone
Have you got our new number?

```
 1 = one
 2 = two
 3 = three
 4 = four
 5 = five
 6 = six
 7 = seven
 8 = eight
 9 = nine
10 = ten
```

nurse

a person whose job is to take care of people who are sick or hurt
Go and see the school nurse, you don't look well.

▲ nurse

nursery (nurseries)

1 a place where babies and small children are cared for during the day
My little brother still goes to a nursery.
2 a place where plants are grown and sold
We bought some beautiful plants at the nursery on the hill.

nursery rhyme

a poem or song for young children
My favorite nursery rhyme is "Jack and Jill."

•Puzzle time•

What are the missing words?

a. Jack and Jill went up the – – – –

b. Humpty – – – – – – sat on a wall

c. Mary, Mary, quite – – – – – – –

d. Little Miss _ _ _ _ _ _ sat on a tuffet

answers
a. hill b. Dumpty c. contrary d. Muffet

nut

a seed that you can eat
Cashews and almonds are different types of nuts.

O o

ocean
1 the salt water that covers most of the Earth
Strange fish live at the bottom of the ocean.
2 a large sea
The Pacific Ocean is the largest ocean.

• Did you know? •
About 97 percent of all the water on Earth is in the oceans. The Pacific is the biggest ocean. It is twice as big as the next largest ocean, the Atlantic. This is followed by the Indian, Southern, and Arctic Oceans.

octopus (octopi)
a sea animal that has eight legs
The legs of the octopus are called tentacles.

▶ **octopus**

off
1 not on
Take the glass off the table.
2 not in use or switched on
Shut the computer down before you switch it off.
3 away from
Keep off the grass.

office
a place where people work at desks
There are 34 people in my Mom's office.

oil
1 a thick liquid made from plants or animals and used for cooking
Put a little olive oil in the pan.
2 a thick liquid that comes out of the ground and is used to make fuel
They discovered oil there last year.
3 a thick liquid that is used on metal or wood so that parts move better or more easily
This door is squeaking. Can you put some oil on it, please?

OK (okay)
1 fine, healthy, well
Are you okay?
2 all right
Is it okay if I copy my work to your computer?

old
not young; not new
My grandpa is getting very old.

▲ **old**

once
1 one time
We've met only once.
2 one time in a fixed period
We go swimming once a week.

onion
a vegetable that has a strong smell and taste
Do you want onions on your pizza?

▶ **onions**

open
not closed or covered over
What time does the store open?

operation
when a doctor cuts open a person's body to mend or remove something
The operation took two hours.

opposite
1 completely different
The opposite of near is far.
2 across from; facing
I sat opposite Dad at the table.

orange
a fruit that grows on trees and is the color between red and yellow

Would you like some orange juice?

◀ orange

orbit (orbiting, orbited)
to travel around and around something, like a planet in space
The Earth orbits the sun.

orchestra
a group of people playing musical instruments together
He plays violin with the school orchestra.

•Puzzle time•

All of these instruments are played in an orchestra. Can you name them all?

a.

b.

c.

d.

a. flute b. drum c. violin d. cello
answers

order
1 to ask for something in a restaurant, or store, or on the Internet
Can I order a soda, please?
2 to tell someone what to do
The captain ordered the men to attack the ship.

ordinary
not special; normal
It's just an ordinary house.

ostrich
a large African bird with a long neck
Ostriches cannot fly.

otter
a brown, furry wild animal that swims and eats fish
Otters are rarely seen.

 ▲ otter

out
1 not in
The mouse got out of his cage.
2 not at home
She's out right now.
3 out of—none left
We're out of sugar.

outdoor
in the open air; not inside a building
I enjoy outdoor sports.

oven
something that you use to bake or roast food
Bake the cake in the oven.

▲ oven

over
1 above; covering
He put a blanket over us.
2 finished; ended
Is the film over yet?
3 from one side to another
A bridge goes over the river.

owl
a bird that hunts at night
Sometimes you can hear an owl hooting.

see also hunt

own (owning, owned)
to have something that you bought or were given
We own a new house.

oxygen
a gas that animals and plants need to live
There is an oxygen mask above your seat.

Pp

pack (packing, packed)
to put things into boxes, bags, or suitcases
Don't forget to pack your bags.

▲ **pack**

package
a small parcel
This package has your name on it.

•Puzzle time•

How many words can you make using the letters from this word?

packages

You should be able to make at least six!

paddle (paddling, paddled)
to move a small boat through water using oars or your hands
They paddled the canoe across the lake.

▼ **paddle**

page
one side of a sheet of paper in a book, magazine, or newspaper
This book has 128 pages.

pain
the feeling you have when you are hurt or ill
I have a bad pain in my side.

paint
a sticky liquid that you brush onto things to color them
Don't spill paint on the carpet.

◀ **paint**

pair
1 two things that go together
I need a new pair of sneakers.
2 something that is made of two similar things joined together
I've bought a new pair of sunglasses for my vacation.

▲ **pair**

•Puzzle time•

Which things do we talk about in pairs? Can you find all the pairs in this picture?

scissors   sneakers
jeans   socks   gloves
answers

palace
a large, very grand house where a king, queen, or other important person lives
The palace is surrounded by beautiful gardens.

▲ palace

palm
1 the inside part of your hand
Fortune tellers read palms.
2 a kind of tree with leaves only at the top
Our tent was under a row of palms on the beach.
see also hand

pan
a round cooking pot that usually has a long handle
Melt the butter in a large pan.

◀ pan

pancake
a thin, flat cake that is cooked in a frying pan
I like pancakes with syrup.

panda
a large black and white animal that looks like a bear
Pandas come from China.

▲ panda

pantomime (mime)
acting something out without using words
He did a pantomime of someone getting dressed.

paper
1 thin sheets of material for writing or printing on
There is no paper in the printer.
2 a newspaper
Mom reads the paper every morning.

parachute
a piece of equipment made of cloth that people wear to let them fall slowly through the air
The parachute will open automatically.

▶ parachute

parade
a number of people walking or marching in a long line to celebrate a special occasion
There is a parade every year.

parent
a mother or father
We're making a special dinner for our parents.

▲ parade

park
a piece of ground with trees and grass, usually in a town
Let's go to the park to play.

park (parking, parked)
to put a car, truck, bus, or bike in a place for a time
You can park right in front of the library.

parrot
a tropical bird with colored feathers
Nadia's parrot can say her name.

▶ **parrot**

part
1 one of the pieces or sections that something is divided into
Would you like part of my orange?
2 the role of an actor in a film or a play
Who is playing the part of the princess?

party (parties)
a group of people gathered together to enjoy themselves
The party is on Saturday.

▼ **party**

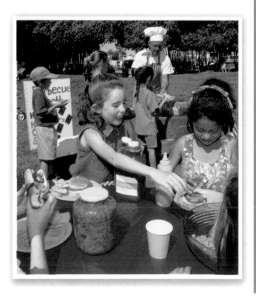

pass (passing, passed)
1 to go beyond or past a person, place, or thing
You'll pass the bakery on your way.
2 to succeed in doing something, such as a test
I hope you pass your driving test.
3 to give someone something
Please pass the strawberries.

passenger
someone who travels in a vehicle that is controlled by someone else
This airplane has seats for 48 passengers.

Passover
a Jewish holiday celebrated in the spring.
The whole family gets together for Passover.
see also holiday

past
1 the time before the present
In the past, there was no such thing as e-mail.
2 up to and beyond
The bank is on this street, just past the supermarket.

pasta
food made from flour, eggs, and water, cut into shapes
Pasta is easy to cook.

▲ **pasta**

paste
a type of glue that is used for sticking paper together
You can make paste with flour and water.

patch (patches)
1 a piece of material to cover a hole in something
I put a patch on my jeans.
2 a small piece of land
We have a vegetable patch in the backyard.

pattern

1 lines, shapes, or colors arranged in a certain way
The pattern on the cushions matches the curtains.
2 a shape that you copy or use as a guide to make something
Mom used a pattern to make this jacket for me.

▲ **pattern**

pause (pausing, paused)

to stop what you are doing for a short time
He paused before carrying on with his speech.

paw

the foot of an animal
Our dog has a sore paw.

pay (paying, paid)

to give someone money for something you are buying, or because someone has done work
I'll pay for their tickets.

pea

a small, round green seed that is eaten as food
Would you like peas with your dinner?

▲ **peas**

peace

1 no war or fighting
There has been peace between them for many years.
2 quiet; calmness
She shut the door for a little peace and quiet.

peach (peaches)

a soft fruit with a large seed inside it
This is a sweet, juicy peach.

▲ **peaches**

peacock

a male bird with long, brightly colored tail feathers that spread out like a fan
Peacocks usually have green and blue feathers.

peanut

a small seed like a nut, inside a soft, bumpy shell
Those peanuts taste very salty.

▲ **peanuts**

pedal

1 part of a bicycle that you push with your feet to make the wheels turn
Can you reach the pedals?
2 part of a car that you push with your feet to make it stop and go
The brake pedal is for stopping the car.

peel (peeling, peeled)

to take the skin off a fruit or a vegetable
I helped peel the potatoes.

pen

an object for drawing and writing with ink
Sign this with a black pen.

▲ **pen**

pencil

an object used for drawing and writing that has lead, not ink, in it
Do the crossword puzzle with a pencil.

◀ **pencils**

penguin

a black and white sea bird
than cannot fly
*Penguins use their wings to help
them swim.*

▼ **penguins**

· Did you know? ·

Penguins usually have one or
two eggs at a time. Both
parents take turns keeping
the eggs warm. Later, the
young penguins are looked
after in groups, usually by the
male bird.

penny

a coin worth one cent
Gumballs cost a penny each.

pepper

1 a hot powder used to
flavor food
Please pass the salt and pepper.
2 a sweet or hot-tasting
vegetable
*Peppers may be green, red,
yellow, or orange.*

▼ **peppers**

perfume

a liquid with a pleasant smell
that you put on your skin
*What perfume are you
wearing?*

permission

to be allowed to do something
*Sam has permission to leave
school early.*

person (people, persons)

a human being—a man,
woman, or child
*Our geography teacher is a
very interesting person.*

pet

an animal that is kept at
someone's home
Do you have any pets?

phone

a telephone
*Could you answer the phone,
please?*

phone (phoning, phoned)

to call someone on the
telephone
Joe phoned while you were out.

photo (photograph)

a picture made with
a camera
*We had our photos taken for
our passports.*

piano

a musical instrument with
black and white keys that you
press to make sounds
A piano has 88 keys.

▶ **piano**

pick (picking, picked)

1 to choose
He was picked for the team.
2 to break off a flower or a
piece of fruit from a plant
We picked some strawberries.
3 to pull pieces off or out of
something
Pick the chicken off the bones.

picnic

food that you take outdoors
to eat
We had a picnic in the park.

▼ **picnic**

picture
a drawing, painting, or photograph
The winner's picture will be in the paper.

pie
food made with fruit, vegetables, or meat that is baked inside pastry
Would you like another piece of pie?

▲ pie

piece
a part of something that has been separated or broken
Careful, there are some pieces of glass on the floor.

pig
a farm animal with pink skin, short legs, a fat body, and a curly tail
A baby pig is called a piglet.

▲ pigs

pile
a lot of things put on top of each other
There's a pile of clothes on the floor.

pillow
a cushion to put your head on in bed
I put my tooth underneath my pillow.

pilot
the person who is in control of a plane
The pilot showed us the plane's control panel.

pin
a sharp, thin piece of metal that is used to fasten things or hold pieces of cloth together
Take all the pins out before you try that on.

pineapple

a brown fruit that is yellow inside and has pointed leaves that stick out of the top
Pineapple juice is sweet.

▲ pineapple

pirate
a person who goes onto boats and ships to steal the things they are carrying
The ship was attacked by a group of pirates.

•Puzzle time•

Where has the pirate buried the treasure? Use the code to find out:

A	B	C	D	E	F	G	H	I	J
1	2	3	4	5	6	7	8	9	10

K	L	M	N	O	P	Q	R
11	12	13	14	15	16	17	18

S	T	U	V	W	X	Y	Z
19	20	21	22	23	24	25	26

21 /14/4/5/18
20/8/5   16/1/12/13
20/18/5/5

answer
under the palm tree

pizza
a thin, flat round bread that is covered with tomatoes, cheese, and other toppings then baked in an oven
We're going to have pizza at the party.

▲ pizza

place

where something is—the position, point, or other location
There is a special place, deep in the forest.

plain

1 one color; having no pattern or decoration
The curtains are plain green.
2 easy to understand
Can you tell me in plain English?
3 not fancy or complicated
It's a plain room, but very clean and neat.

plan

1 an idea about what will happen in the future
We have vacation plans.
2 a drawing of a room, building, or other space
We drew a plan for our perfect playground.

plan (planning, planned)

to think about what you want to do and how to do it
We're planning a party.

plane

an airplane
The plane took off from the airport on time.

planet

one of the very large, round objects that moves around the sun
There are nine planets in our solar system.

Pluto

Neptune

Uranus

Saturn

Jupiter

Earth

Mars

Mercury

Venus

▲ **planets**

plant (planting, planted)

to put seeds or plants into the ground or in containers so that they will grow
Plant the seeds in early summer.

plant

a living thing that has roots, leaves, and seeds and can make its own food
Water the plant every day.

plaster

a very thick paste that hardens when it dries
Plaster is used to cover walls inside buildings.

plastic
a light material that is made from chemicals
The bucket is made of plastic.

plate
a flat dish to eat food from
Take the plates into the kitchen.

▲ **plates**

play
a story performed by actors in a theater or on the radio
The Tempest is a play full of magical things.

play (playing, played)
to do things that you like, such as games or sports
Let's play outside.

▲ **play**

playground
a place for children to play
There are swings and a slide at the playground.

please
a word to use when you are asking for something politely
Please wait here.

plenty
enough or more than enough
Have one of my sandwiches, I have plenty.

plow
a piece of equipment that farmers use to turn the soil before they plant
Modern plows can cut through the soil very quickly.

▲ **plow**

plug
1 a piece of plastic or rubber that stops water from going out of a sink or bathtub
Put the plug in the bathtub, then turn on the water.
2 a piece of plastic connected to an electrical wire that you put into a wall
Which one is the plug for the computer?

plumber
a person whose job is to fix water faucets and pipes
The plumber repaired the leak.

plus (pluses)
and; added to; the symbol +
Eleven plus six equals seventeen.

$$11 + 6 = 17$$

 ◀ **plus**

pocket
a small, flat bag sewn into a piece of clothing or luggage
Put your key in your pocket.

poem
writing that uses words that sound good together. The words may rhyme
This poem is very funny.

•Puzzle time•
Here is a scrambled poem. Can you put each line in the correct order?
Hint—each line begins with a word that has a capital letter.

a. Roses red are
b. are blue Violets
c. sweet is Sugar
d. And are you so

noʎ os puɐ puɐ ˙p
ʇǝǝʍs sᴉ ɹɐƃnS ˙ɔ
ǝnlq ǝɹɐ sʇǝloᴉΛ ˙q
pǝɹ ǝɹɐ sǝsoꓤ ˙ɐ
sɹǝʍsuɐ

point

1 a sharp end on something
Use a pencil with a sharp point.
2 a certain place or time
There's a meeting point at the airport.
3 the reason for something
The whole point was to raise money for the school.
4 a mark for counting a score in a game
The answer is worth one point.

point (pointing, pointed)

to use your hand or finger to show someone something
Point to where the gate is

pole

1 a long, narrow piece of wood, plastic, or metal
We forgot to take the tent poles.

police

people whose job is to make everyone obey the law
Police officers work very hard.

polite

speaking or acting in a pleasant and not rude way
It is polite to say please, thank you, and excuse me.

pond

a small area of water
There are fish in the pond.

pony (ponies)

a small horse
Dusty is a beautiful little pony.

▲ **pony**

pool

1 a place filled with water for swimming
I like playing in my pool when the weather is warm.
2 a puddle or another small area of water
We saw tiny, colored fish in the pools on the beach.

▲ **pool**

poor

1 not having enough money
It's a very poor country.
2 not as good as it should be
The food was poor.

pop

1 a sudden noise
There was a loud pop when they opened the bottle.
2 a short form of "popular"
They are a very famous pop band.

porcupine

a wild animal with long needles on its back
Porcupine needles are called quills.

▼ **porcupine**

pork

meat from a pig
We're having pork chops for dinner tonight.

possible

something that might happen, or could be done.
It is possible that we will arrive on time for the show.

post office

a place where people buy stamps and send letters.
Can you get me some stamps at the post office?

potato (potatoes)
a roundish, white vegetable
that grows under the ground
*Potatoes have brown, yellow,
or red skins.*

◄ **potatoes**

pour (pouring, poured)
to make a liquid
move out of or into
something
*Pour the juice while
I make breakfast.*

► **pour**

powerful
1 having strength
A crocodile has powerful jaws.
2 able to control
*It is one of the most powerful
countries in the world.*

practice
something you do again and
again to improve a skill
*What time is swimming
practice tonight?*

**practice (practicing,
practiced)**
doing something regularly to
improve a skill
Keep practicing your serve.

praise (praising, praised)
to say good things about
someone
*Dad praised the police for
acting so quickly.*

**prepare (preparing,
prepared)**
to get ready, or to make
something ready
I'm preparing for the test.

present   ▼ **present**
1 a gift; a thing
that you
are given
without
asking for it
*Thank you for
all the presents.*
2 now
The story is set in the present.

president
the leader of an organization
or a country
She is president of the club.

press (pressing, pressed)
to push something
Press the space bar.

**pretend (pretending,
pretended)**
to act like something is true
when it is not
She pretended to be asleep.

pretty
pleasant to look at
What pretty flowers!

price
the amount of money that
a thing costs
The prices are high.

prince
the son or grandson of a king
or queen
*Prince Charming found the
glass slipper.*

princess (princesses)
a daughter or the
granddaughter of
a king or queen
*The princess dreamed
of a faraway place.*

▲ **princess**

print (printing, printed)
1 to put letters, numbers, or pictures on paper with a machine
Print five copies of the story.
2 to write words without joining the letters together
Print your name.

printer
1 a machine connected to a computer that makes copies on paper
The printer is out of paper.
2 a person who runs a printing machine
Take the poster to the printer.

prison
a place where people are kept under guard as punishment
The thief was sent to prison.

prize
something that you win in a game or contest
The first prize is a vacation.

problem
1 something that is wrong and needs to be corrected
We have a problem with this floppy disk.
2 a question that needs to be answered
There are 25 problems in the math test.

promise (promising, promised)
to tell someone that you will definitely do something
The boy promised he would be good.

protect (protecting, protected)
to take care of someone or something and not let it be hurt or damaged
The penguin protects its chick from danger.

▲ **protect**

proud
feeling pleased or happy that you or someone else has done something or has something
Her parents were very proud of her.

puddle
a little pool of water on the ground or floor
There were puddles on the sidewalk after the rain.

pull (pulling, pulled)
to move something toward you in a certain direction or to drag something behind you
We pulled on the rope as hard as we could.

▲ **pull**

pump
a machine that moves a liquid or gas in a certain direction
Take your tire pump with you in case you have a puncture.

punch (punching, punched)
to hit something hard with your fist
A boxer can punch very hard.

punish (punishing, punished)
to do something bad or unpleasant to someone because they have done something wrong
Don't punish him, it was an accident.

pupil

1 a school student
The pupils at our school wear uniforms.
2 the black center of your eye
Your pupil gets smaller when you look at a bright light.
see also eye

puppet

a toy that people move by putting their hand inside it or by pulling strings attached to it
There's a puppet show starting in 10 minutes.

▲ **puppet**

puppy (puppies)

a young dog
Puppies open their eyes when they are about two weeks old.

▲ **puppies**

purchase (purchasing, purchased)

to buy something
We've purchased a new car.

pure

not mixed with anything else
This is pure apple juice.

purpose

a reason or intention behind something
The purpose of the test is to see how well you can spell.

purr

the soft, low sound a cat makes when it is happy
Our cat purrs when you scratch his ears.

push (pushing, pushed)

1 to move something away from you or out of your way
He pushed past everyone.
2 to press down on something, such as a key or a button
Push the restart button.

put (putting, put)

to move a thing to a place
Just put the bags over there.

pyramid

1 a very old stone building with triangular walls that form a point at the top
The Egyptian pyramids were built 4,000 years ago.
2 something with this shape
The tent is pyramid-shaped.

▲ **pyramids**

• **Did you know?** •
It took 20,000 men more than 20 years to build the great Egyptian pyramids!

python

a large snake that kills animals for food by squeezing them
Some pythons grow to be 25 feet (8 meters) long.

◄ **python**

Qq

quarter
one of four equal, or nearly equal, parts of something
Divide the apple into quarters.

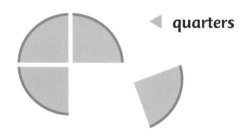

◀ **quarters**

queen
the royal female ruler of a country, or the wife of a king
The queen lives in a palace.

◀ **queen**

question
something that you ask someone
We'll try to answer all your questions.

quick (quickly)
fast
E-mail is quick and easy.

quiet (quietly)
1 not making noise
Please be quiet.
2 calm and still; not busy
The lake is quiet and peaceful.

quilt
a warm cover for a bed
Patchwork quilts are made by sewing lots of small pieces of cloth together.

▲ **quilt**

quit (quitting)
to stop doing something or to leave a computer program
To quit, press Ctrl + Q.

quite
more than a little but not very much
The weather is quite warm.

quiz
a game or competition that tests your knowledge
There is a quiz at school today.

•Puzzle time•
Can you answer all the questions in this quiz?
Hint—the answers are all in this dictionary.
a. What is a baby pig called?
b. Can penguins fly?
c. Is a tomato a fruit or a vegetable?
d. What are the needles on a porcupine called?
e. How many hours are there in a day?

a. piglet b. no c. a fruit
d. quills e. 24
answers

quote (quoting, quoted)
to repeat the words that someone else has said or written
The English teacher quoted a line from Shakespeare's Hamlet to the class.

Rr

rabbit

a small furry animal with long ears
There are rabbits living in the woods.

▲ **rabbits**

race

1 a competition to see who can do something fastest
The race starts in 15 minutes.
2 a group of people with similar physical features
The goal is that people of all races and all beliefs can live together happily.

race (racing, raced)

1 to compete in a race
They're racing against some of the fastest runners in the world.
2 to do something very quickly
Jessie raced through the first part of the test.

racket (racquet)

1 a flat, hard net at the end of a stick, which you use to play sports such as tennis, badminton, and squash
These new tennis rackets are very light.
2 noise
Who's making that racket?

▲ **racket**

•Puzzle time•

Which of these sports is played with a racket?

a. tennis   **b.** golf

c. baseball   **d.** squash

answers
a and d

▲ **radio**

radio

a piece of equipment that receives sounds from the air
I listen to music on my radio.

rail

1 a bar used to support or to stop things from falling
Hold on to the rail when you walk across the bridge.
2 one of two metal tracks that a train runs on
They put new rails all along the track.

railroad

1 a train track
The railroad runs to the coast.
2 a system of trains
A light railroad is being built in the city.

rain

water that falls from clouds in the sky
All the rain left lots of puddles.

rainbow

the curve of colors that you see in the sky after it rains and the sun comes out
The colors of the rainbow are red, orange, yellow, green, blue, indigo, and violet.

▶ **rainbow**

raise (raising, raised)
to lift or put something in a higher place
Raise your hand if you know the answer.

rat
an animal that looks like a big mouse with a long tail
There are rats in the barn.

▲ **rat**

rattle
a toy that makes a knocking noise when you shake it
Babies like rattles because they make noise.

raw
not cooked
You can cook cabbage or eat it raw.

read (reading, read)
to understand words or symbols printed on a page
I like reading in the garden.

▲ **read**

record (recording, recorded)
to write down, tape, or otherwise store information
We recorded our voices on the computer.

recycle (recycling, recycled)
to use something over again
We're recycling newspapers and magazines at school.

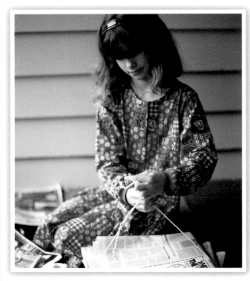

▲ **recycle**

reflection
an image, like a copy of something, that is seen in a mirror or water
We could see the reflection of the mountain in the water.

▼ **reflection**

refrigerator (fridge)
a machine to keep food cool
Put the milk back in the refrigerator.

▲ **refrigerator**

remember (remembering, remembered)
1 to keep information about the past in your mind
I remember how much fun we had then.
2 to bring back information to your mind
Oh! I just remembered—we're supposed to phone Gina!

remind (reminding, reminded)
to cause someone to remember something
Remind me to buy sugar.

repeat (repeating, repeated)
to say or do something again
Sorry, could you repeat that—I didn't hear you.

rescue (rescuing, rescued)
to save someone or
something from danger
*The lifeguard rescued the
children.*

rest (resting, rested)
to not be active; to relax
I wasn't asleep, just resting.

restaurant
a place where people eat and
pay for meals
*There's a new Thai restaurant
in town.*

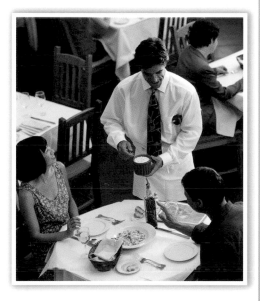

▲ **restaurant**

result
something that happens
because of something else
*This beautiful garden is the
result of a lot of hard work.*

return (returning, returned)
1 to come back or go back to
a place
He returned after the meeting.
2 to give or send something
back
*We returned the books to the
library.*

rhinoceros
(rhinoceroses)
a very large, wild
animal with thick
skin and a large
horn on its nose
*Rhinoceroses have
very weak eyesight.*

▲ **rhinoceros**

rhyme (rhyming, rhymed)
when a word ends with the
same sound as another word
Tree rhymes with three.

•Puzzle time•

Which words in column A
rhyme with words in column B?

A	B
book	hard
card	boat
coat	look
cow	other
mother	so
sew	now

answers
book/look, card/hard,
coat/boat, cow/now,
mother/other, sew/so

ribbon
a narrow piece of
cloth or paper for
tying up presents
or decorating
things ▲ **ribbon**
*What color ribbon
should we put on her present?*

rice
grains from a plant that are
boiled and eaten as food
*We had rice with our
vegetable curry.*

▲ **rice**

rich
1 having a lot of money
*We are not rich, but we're
very happy.*
2 food that has butter,
cream, and eggs is rich food
The sauce is too rich for me!
3 a deep or strong color,
smell, or sound
*The queen is wearing rich,
purple robes.*

riddle
a difficult but funny question
Tom knows lots of riddles.

ride (riding, rode, ridden)

to travel on and control the movement of a bicycle or a horse
She is learning to ride a bike.

▲ ride

right

correct
Very good—you got all the answers right!

ring

1 a piece of jewelry worn on the finger
It's a pretty silver ring.
2 a circle or something that is the shape of a circle
We put our chairs in a ring around the teacher.
3 the sound made by a bell
The phone has a very loud ring.
4 a telephone call
Give me a ring when you get home from work.

river

a long line of water that flows to the ocean
The longest river in the world is the Nile.

road

a track for vehicles such as cars and trucks to travel on
Some country roads are very narrow.

roar

the sound a lion makes
There was a loud roar right outside the tent.

▲ roar

robot

a machine that can do things that a person can do
My robot can play soccer.

◄ robot

rock

1 the hard, stony part of the Earth's surface
They drilled through rock to find the oil.
2 a large stone
We sat on the rocks and fished.
3 a type of music that has a strong beat
My brother likes hard rock.

rocket

1 a space vehicle shaped like a tube
The rocket is carrying valuable equipment to the space station.
2 a tube-shaped firework
Rockets were exploding all over the sky.

▼ rocket

roll (rolling, rolled)

to move by turning over
The ball rolled across the field.

roof

the outer covering over the top of a building or car
Rain leaked through the roof and onto the floor.

room

part of a building that has its own floor, walls, and ceiling
What's your room like?

rope

very thick string
Tie the rope as tight as you can.

▶ rope

rose

a flower that grows on a stem with thorns
My mother loves roses.

▲ **roses**

rough

1 uneven, not smooth
That bench is very rough.
2 not gentle
Don't be so rough with the puppy.

round

something that is shaped like a circle or a ball
Most coins are round.

route

the way to go to a place
We looked at the map and decided which route we should take.

row (rowing, rowed)

to move a boat through water using long poles that are wide at one end
We rowed the boat across the lake.

royal

of or belonging to a queen or king
The royal palace is in the heart of the city.

rubber

a bouncy, stretchy material that is made from the juice of a tree
Car tires are made from rubber.

rude

speaking or acting in such a way that makes other people feel badly
It's rude to whisper.

rug

a small carpet
The dog is asleep on a rug.

ruin (ruining, ruined)

1 to spoil something
Bad weather ruined their wedding day.
2 a very rundown building, such a house
The house was now a complete ruin.

rule

a law or a guide about how something must be done
It's wrong to break the rules at school.

ruler

1 a long, flat piece of plastic or wood that has a straight edge and measurements on it
Use a ruler to draw a line.
2 a person who has power over a country
The country had no ruler when the king died.

▶ **ruler**

run (running, ran)

1 to move your legs faster than when you are walking
Run as fast as you can!
2 to control
He runs his own business.
3 to make a piece of equipment or a computer program work
Run the computer program.

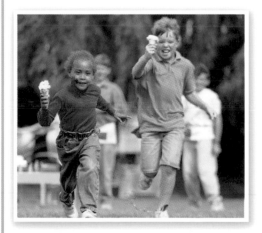

▲ **run**

• Did you know? •
The fastest human being can run at an amazing 23 miles (37 kilometers) per hour!

Ss

sad
unhappy
What's happened? You look so sad.

safe
not dangerous
Home is where you feel good and safe.

sail
a large piece of strong material attached to a boat or ship, which catches the wind and makes the boat move across the water
The ship has many sails.

▼ sails

sail (sailing, sailed)
to travel across water in a boat or ship
I am learning to sail a boat.

salad
vegetables or fruit mixed together, usually eaten raw
We'll have a mixed salad.

▼ salad

salt
very tiny grains that come from sea water and rocks, which are put on food to make it taste good
This needs a little more salt.

same
not different or changed
Look, our clothes are exactly the same.

sand
tiny pieces of crushed rock
The beach is covered in beautiful, white sand.

sandwich (sandwiches)
two pieces of bread with cheese, meat, or vegetables in between
We'll make some sandwiches for the picnic.

▼ sandwich

•Puzzle time•
Can you put these sandwich instructions in the correct order?
a. Next, spread one side of each slice with butter.
b. Put the cheese on one slice of bread.
c. Now put the other slice on top.
d. How to make a cheese sandwich.
e. First take two slices of bread.
f. Eat your sandwich.

answer
d e b c f

saucer
the small dish that goes under a cup
We put some milk in a saucer for the kittens.

sausage
a mixture of meat, cereal, and spices that is shaped like a tube
Would you like sausages with your breakfast?

scale
a machine that is used for weighing things
Weigh the flour on the scale.

◀ scale

a b c d e f g h i j k l m

scar

the mark left on your skin after a cut has healed
I have a scar above my left eye.

scare (scaring, scared)

to frighten
The film will scare you.

scared

feeling afraid, frightened
Please leave a light on, I'm scared of the dark.

scarecrow

an object made to look like a person that is put in fields to scare birds off so they don't eat the crops
Our scarecrow is made of straw.

school

the place where children go to study and be taught
I'm learning to speak French at school.

science

the study of information about the world
Biology, physics, and chemistry are all kinds of science.

score (scoring, scored)

to get points in a game
We've scored another goal!

scorpion

an animal that has eight legs and a tail
Scorpions have a painful sting.

▲ **scorpion**

• **Did you know?** •

Scorpions have been on Earth for a very long time—about 4 million years!

scratch (scratching, scratched)

1 to rub your skin with your fingers or nails
Don't scratch your face.
2 to damage an object by rubbing it with something
The stones scratched the car.

scream (screaming, screamed)

to make a loud noise when you are afraid, angry, or hurt
She screamed loudly.

screen

1 the flat part of a computer or television that you look at
You're too close to the screen.
2 a flat piece of material for showing films on
The movie's on a wide screen.

sea

a large area of salty water, sometimes called the ocean
Look, you can see the sea from here.

seal

1 an animal that lives in the ocean and eats fish
Seals are good swimmers and can stay underwater for a long time.
2 wax, plastic, or paper that you break to open a container or a document
Do not buy this product if the seal is broken.

▲ **seals**

• **Did you know?** •

Seals can be found in all the world's oceans. They are fast swimmers and skillful hunters of fish and squid, although the leopard seal hunts mainly penguins. Seals can dive to great depths and stay underwater for long periods of time. Lake Baikal, in Siberia, Russia, is a huge inland lake, and is home to the world's only freshwater seals.

secret
something that you do not want other people to know
Please don't tell anyone else— it's a secret.

see (seeing, saw, seen)
1 to use your eyes to look
We saw a deer.
2 to understand
See? This is how it works.
3 to watch
Did you see that TV show last night?
4 to meet or visit someone
We went to see Chloe in the hospital.

seed
the part of a plant that a new plant grows from
Put the seeds in the ground and water them.

▼ **seeds**

seesaw
a long board that is balanced in the middle so that the ends go up and down
There's a seesaw in the playground.

send (sending, sent)
to make something go or be taken to another place
I sent her an e-mail yesterday.

sew (sewing, sewed, sewn)
to join cloth together with a needle and thread
I'll sew the button on for you.

shade
1 where the sun is not shining
Sit in the shade of the umbrella.
2 a thing to stop light
Pull the shades down.
3 a color
That's a nice shade of green.

▲ **shade**

shake (shaking, shook, shaken)
to move something up and down or side to side quickly
Shake well before opening.

shampoo
soap for washing your hair
Did you bring the shampoo?

shape
the outline or form of a thing
What shape is it?

shark
a large fish with sharp teeth
Some sharks can be dangerous to humans.

▼ **sharks**

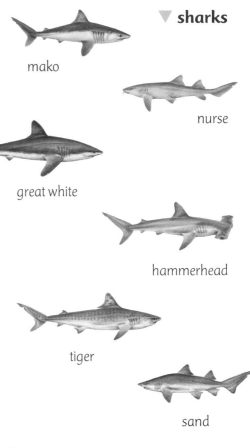

mako

nurse

great white

hammerhead

tiger

sand

sheep (sheep)
a farm animal kept for wool and meat
There are sheep on the hill.

▲ **sheep**

shelf (shelves)
a board fixed on a wall, or in a piece of furniture, for putting things on
Can you reach that shelf?

shell
the hard covering of an egg, a seed, or an animal, such as a turtle or a crab
Ostrich eggs are very big and have thick shells.

ship
a large boat
The pirates filled the ship with treasure.

▼ **ship**

mizzen topsail
main topsail
mainsail
fore topsail
foresail

stern
sail locker
water and supplies
oar
bow
bowsprit

• Did you know? •
Pirate ships were small, but fast. This meant they could make a quick getaway with stolen treasure.

shirt
a piece of clothing worn on the top half of your body
Tuck your shirt in.

shock
1 a bad surprise
The bill was quite a shock.
2 a pain you feel when electricity goes through your body
I got a shock from that plug!

shoe
one of the things made of strong material that you wear on your feet
Wear comfortable shoes.

shoot (shooting, shot)
1 to fire a weapon at someone or something
Don't shoot!
2 to kick or throw a ball into a goal or net in a game
Shoot when you are closer to the basket.

shop (shopping, shopped)
to buy something in a store
I love shopping for clothes!

short
1 not tall
He is short for his age.
2 not long
She cut her hair short.
3 not lasting a long time
Let's take a short break.

shorts
short pants
We wear shorts in the summer.

▲ **shorts**

shoulder
the top of your arm where it joins your body
Put the bag over your shoulder.

shout (shouting, shouted)
to call out in a loud voice
Don't shout, I'm right here!

show (showing, showed)
1 to let someone see something
Show me your new game.
2 to guide someone somewhere or help them to do something
The guide showed us around.

shower
1 a thing that you stand under to wash your body
Every room has a private shower.
2 a light fall of rain
There will be showers in the afternoon.

shrink (shrinking, shrank, shrunk)
to become smaller
My favorite skirt shrank in the wash.

shut (shutting, shut)
to close
Shut the door, please.

sideways
toward one side, not forward or backward
Turn sideway,s and then you can get past.

sign (signing, signed)
to write your name on something
Sign at the bottom.

silly
stupid; not reasonable
Don't be silly!

sing (singing, sang, sung)
to make music with your voice
Sing us a song.

sink (sinking, sank, sunk)
to go down below the surface of water
The Titanic sank after it hit an iceberg.

▲ sink

sister
a girl or woman who has the same parents as you
Julie is my younger sister.

sit (sitting, sat)
to put your bottom on a chair or another type of seat
I must sit down, my feet ache.

skate (skating, skated)
to move over ground or ice wearing boots with wheels or blades
He can skate well.

▲ skate

skeleton
the bones in your body
He wore a suit with a skeleton painted on it for Halloween.

sketch (sketching, sketched)
to draw quickly
Artists sketch a scene first.

ski (skiing, skied)
to move quickly over snow or water on long, narrow pieces of wood
Do you know how to ski?

▲ ski

skirt
a piece of clothing worn by girls and women that hangs from the waist down
You can wear that skirt to school.

sky (skies)
the space above you where the sun, moon, stars, and clouds are
The sky was full of stars.

slap (slapping, slapped)
to hit something with an open hand
She slapped his hand.

sled
a vehicle or toy for moving across ice or snow
We built a sled out of an old wooden box.

sleep (sleeping, slept)
to not be awake
The baby is sleeping in his crib.

▲ sleep

slide (sliding, slid)
to move across or down a smooth surface
The car slid across the ice.

slippers
shoes that you wear indoors
Put your slippers on if your feet are cold.

slow
not fast; taking a long time
This is a slow train.

small
little or young
The jeans have a small pocket for coins.

smile (smiling, smiled)
to make your mouth curve up and look happy
What are you smiling about?

▲ smile

smoke
the cloudy gas that is made when something burns
The room filled with smoke.

smooth
not rough or bumpy
You can skate on the sidewalk, because it's smooth.

snail
an animal that looks like a worm with a shell on its back
We have a lot of snails in our garden.

▶ snail

· Did you know? ·
The largest snail is the African giant snail. The biggest ever recorded was the size of a soccer ball!

snake
an animal that has a long body with no legs
Simon has a pet snake.

▲ snake

sneeze (sneezing, sneezed)
to blow air out of your nose suddenly, with a loud noise
He's sneezing and coughing because he has a cold.

snow
soft pieces of frozen water that fall from the sky
The trees are covered with snow.

▲ **snow**

soap
something that you use with water to wash your body
Get a new bar of soap.

▲ **soap**

soccer
a game played by two teams that try to kick a ball between two goal posts
There are 11 players on a soccer team.

▲ **soccer**

socks
soft pieces of clothing that you wear inside shoes
Socks keep your feet warm.

◄ **socks**

sofa
a long, soft seat for two or more people
Let's sit on the sofa.

soft
1 not hard
These apples are a little soft.
2 not loud
She has a soft voice.
3 smooth to touch
The rabbit has nice, soft fur.

software
the programs that run on a computer
He designs software.

solid
hard; not a liquid or a gas; without spaces inside
The front door is solid wood.

some
1 an amount that is not exact
Do you want some rice?
2 part of, but not all
Some of these apples are rotten.

son
a male child
His son is my age.

song
a piece of music
Let's all sing a song.

sore
hurting or painful
Is your leg still sore?

sorry
feeling bad and wanting to apologize for something you have done
I'm sorry I upset you.

soup
a liquid food made from meat or vegetables
Have a bowl of tomato soup.

► **soup**

sour
having a taste like lemons; not sweet
This juice is sour.

space
1 an empty or open place
Is there any space left?
2 everything outside the Earth's air
Space travel is very exciting.

spade
a tool for digging
Turn over the soil with a spade.

spaghetti
long, thin strips of pasta
Ella likes spaghetti.

▲ **spaghetti**

speed
how fast something moves
At what speed are we traveling?

spell (spelling, spelled)
to write or say the letters of
a word in the correct order
How do you spell "skateboard?"

spider
a small animal with
eight legs
*There's a spider in
the bathtub.*

▶ **spider**

spill (spilling, spilled, spilt)
to cause a liquid to fall to the
ground accidentally
I spilled the drink on the carpet.

spoon
an object with a handle and
small bowl that is used
for eating
*Put the spoon to
the right of the
plate.*

▲ **spoon**

sports
physical activities, such as
swimming and tennis
*Swimming is a sport the
whole family likes.*

snowboarding

spring
the time of year between
winter and summer
*The cherry tree flowers
in the spring.*

squirrel
a small wild animal with
a long, bushy tail
*Squirrels are very good
at climbing trees.*

▼ **sports**

hockey

gymnastics

·Puzzle time·
Can you unscramble the names
of these sports?

a. seablabl **b.** gsmwmin
c. cykeoh **d.** nintes **e.** ftbllooa

answers
a. baseball b. swimming
c. hockey d. tennis e. football

volleyball

stairs
steps in a building that go from one floor to another
I'll walk up the stairs to the office.

stamp
a small piece of paper that you buy to put on a letter or postcard before you mail it
I'd like a 37-cent stamp.

stand (standing, stood)
to be on your feet
She's standing by the main entrance.

star
1 a ball of burning gas that looks like a light in the sky
The stars are very bright tonight.
2 a famous actor or musician
She's a big star now.
3 a shape with five or six points
We baked cookies shaped like stars

starfish (starfishes)
a star-shaped animal that lives in the sea
Starfish move very slowly.

◄ starfish

start (starting, started)
to begin
Ready? Let's start.

stay (staying, stayed)
1 to not leave a place
You stay here, I'll be right back.
2 to live in a place for a short amount of time
We stayed with my aunt for a week.
3 to continue to be the same
Stay happy!

steal (stealing, stole, stolen)
to take something that doesn't belong to you
The thief stole my dad's car.

white dwarf

supernova

◄ stars

stick
a long, thin piece of wood
We made a fire by rubbing two sticks together.

stomach
the part inside your body where food goes when you eat it
My stomach rumbles when I'm hungry.

food pipe

stomach

large intestine

small intestine

▲ stomach

stone
1 rock
There is a stone floor in the castle.
2 the seed in some fruits such as cherries, peaches, and plums
Careful, the cherries have stones in them.

stool
a seat with no back or arms
We sit on stools in the art room.

stop (stopping, stopped)
1 to quit doing something
Stop talking for a minute.
2 to quit moving
You should stop for red lights.
3 to prevent something from happening
The teacher stopped the fight.

story (stories)
a description of events that may be real or imaginary
Everyone knows the story of Peter Pan.

• Did you know? •
The story of Peter Pan was first written by J.M. Barrie in 1902. Peter Pan was the hero in a novel called *The Little White Bird*. The story was then adapted for a play in 1904 called *Peter Pan*. In the play Peter flies away to Never Never Land to avoid growing up. Other famous characters are the Darlings, Captain Hook, and Tiger Lily.

straight
not crooked or bent
She has very straight hair.

strange
1 unusual
That's a strange-looking man.
2 unfamiliar
We were in a strange town.

strawberry
(strawberries)
a soft, heart-shaped, red fruit
You can pick the strawberries yourself on some farms.

▼ **strawberries**

stream
a small river
We drank water from a mountain stream.

stretch (stretching, stretched)
1 to get longer or bigger
My gloves stretched when my dad wore them.
2 to straighten parts of your body
She stretched her legs out under the table.

string
thick thread or thin rope
Tie some string around the box.

▲ **string**

strong
1 powerful
Climbers have strong legs.
2 not easily broken or damaged
The metal case is very strong.

stupid
not sensible
What a stupid idea!

submarine
a ship that can travel underwater
Submarines can help us find out about underwater life.

▲ **submarine**

sudden
happening quickly and unexpectedly
There was a sudden explosion.

sugar
a sweet substance used to flavor food
Sugar is made from plants.

suitcase
a case or bag to carry clothes in when you travel
We have a suitcase with wheels.

summer
the time of year between spring and fall
Are you going on vacation this summer?

sun
the very bright star that the Earth travels around
All the planets in the solar system travel around the sun.

▼ **sun**

supermarket
a large store that sells food and other things
The supermarket is open.

surprise
something that is completely unexpected
An e-mail from you! What a nice surprise!

sweep (sweeping, swept)
to brush dirt from the floor or ground
Have you swept the kitchen?

sweet
1 tasting sugary
These strawberries are very sweet.
2 nice or pleasant
That's a sweet thing to say.

swim (swimming, swam, swum)
to move through or across water by using your arms and legs
I can swim a whole length of the pool.

▲ **swim**

swing (swinging, swung)
to move backward, forward or from side to side from a fixed point
I like swinging—it's lots of fun.

▲ **swing**

sword
a very large knife that is used for fighting
"Excalibur" is the name of a famous sword.

▶ **sword**

Tt

T-shirt/t-shirt
a shirt with short sleeves, no collar, and no buttons
Put a T-shirt on.

table
1 a piece of furniture with legs and a flat top
Please clear the table.
2 a list of things, such as numbers or words, arranged in rows and columns
There's a table of prices and times.

▲ table

tail
the part of an animal at the end of its back
The dog has a long, white tail.

▶ tail

take (taking, took, taken)
1 to carry something
Take an umbrella.
2 to move something or someone to another place
Take this note to Mrs. Burnett.
3 to steal
The thieves took all the money.

talk (talking, talked)
to speak
Whom were you talking to?

tall
1 higher than normal
My grandpa is tall; I am short.
2 having a certain height
The fence is 3 feet (1 meter) tall.

◀ tall

tangle
something that is twisted or knotted together
My hair is in a tangle.

tank
1 a container for liquids
There's a leak in the gas tank.
2 a large fighting vehicle
Tanks are used in wars.

tape
1 a long, flat, narrow piece of plastic used for recording sounds or images, or the plastic container it is in
Can I borrow the tape?
2 flat, narrow plastic that is sticky on one side
Put some tape on the package.

taste (tasting, tasted)
1 to have a flavor
What does the soup taste like?
2 to try a little food or drink to see what it is like
Have you tasted the pizza?

taxi
a car that takes people places for money
We'll take a taxi.

▼ taxi

tea
leaves that are used to make a drink, or the drink made from these leaves
Pour the tea.

teacher

a person who gives lessons in a subject
Kate's an art teacher.

team

1 a group of people who play a game together
Which team are you on?
2 a group of people who work together on a project
We have a great team.

▲ **team**

tear

a drop of water that comes out of your eye
Tears ran down his face.

tear (tearing, tore, torn)

to rip, split, or make a hole in something
Tear the paper in half.

teddy bear

a toy animal that looks like a bear
My teddy bear is soft and cuddly.

▲ **teddy bear**

telephone

a piece of equipment that you use to speak to someone in another place
Where's your telephone?

▲ **telephone**

telescope

a piece of equipment that you use to look at things that are far away
Look through the telescope.

•Puzzle time•

Can you match the names of these star patterns to the correct picture?
1. Pegasus (winged horse)
2. Ursa Major (Great Bear)
3. Hercules
4. Orion (Hunter)

a

b

c

d

answers
1b 2a 3d 4c

television (TV)

a machine that shows programs
What's on television?

viewfinder

eyepiece

object lens

telescope tube

▲ **telescope**

tell (telling, told)
1 to pass on information
I told you that story yesterday.
2 to understand
I can't tell what it means.

tennis
a game played by two or four people who hit a ball over a net to score points
Tennis is a very fast game.

▲ **tennis**

tent
a temporary house, made of cloth or plastic that is used for camping
The tent will keep us dry.

terrible
very bad
That's terrible!

test
1 a set of questions to measure knowledge
You must study carefully for the test.
2 a set of checks to find out if something is safe or good to use
Cars must pass several tests.

thank (thanking, thanked)
to tell someone you are pleased about something they have given you or have done for you
Remember to thank them.

theater
a building where you can go and see plays
We have tickets for the theater.

thick
1 not thin
The phone book is thick.
2 not watery
Make a thick paste from flour and water.

thief (thieves)
a person who steals
The thieves stole all the money from the bank.

thin
1 having not much distance from one side to the other
Cut thin strips of paper.
2 not fat
She's very thin.
3 watery
It's a thin, clear soup.

think (thinking, thought)
1 to use your mind to consider or remember something
Let me think.
2 to have an opinion; to believe
I think we should try it.

thirsty
feeling that you need to drink something
Are you thirsty?

through
from one side to the other
Look through the window.

throw (throwing, threw)
to make something go through the air
Throw the ball through the hoop.

thumb
the finger on the inside of your hand
Use your thumb to hit the space bar on the keyboard.

thunder
the loud noise during a storm
*We heard a very loud clap
of thunder.*

ticket
a piece of paper that shows
you have paid
*Tickets are half-price for
children.*

tidy
neat and organized
Mandy's room is never tidy.

·Puzzle time·

Can you find six differences
between these two rooms?

answers
1 crumpled paper **2** spilled ink
3 sock **4** teddy bear **5** unmade bed
6 closet door

tie (tying, tied)
to join pieces of string, rope,
or thread together
Tie your shoelaces.

tiger
a large wild cat that has black
stripes on its yellow fur
Tigers are the biggest wild cats.

▼ **tiger**

· Did you know? ·
Tigers are the biggest cats, but there
are few left in the wild. Overhunting
and destruction of their habitat has
made them very rare.

tight
1 close-fitting
That looks a little tight.
2 firmly in place
Is it shut tight?

tights
clothing worn on the legs
I wear tights to ballet.

timetable
a list of things and the times
they happen
Check the timetable.

tired
feeling that you need to rest
The baby is tired.

toast
bread that has been browned
in a toaster or on a grill
*I'll make some toast for
breakfast.*

▲ **toast**

today
this day
What's the date today?

toe
one of the five parts of your
body at the end of your foot
Ouch! I stubbed my toe.

together
1 joined or mixed
Mix the eggs and milk together.
2 with each other
Let's go together.

toilet
The flushable bowl you use
when you go to the bathroom
Please flush the toilet.

tomato (tomatoes)
a red fruit that
can be eaten
raw or
cooked
*Put tomatoes
in the salad.* ▲ **tomatoes**

tool
a piece of equipment that you use to do a job
Hammers and saws are tools.

tooth (teeth)
one of the hard, white things in your mouth
You should brush your teeth twice a day.

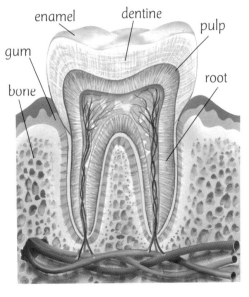

enamel
dentine
pulp
gum
bone
root

▲ **tooth**

tongue
the soft part of your body inside your mouth, which you use to speak with and to taste things
The ice cream feels cold on my tongue.

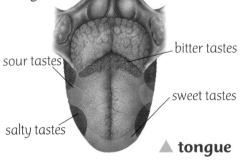

sour tastes
bitter tastes
sweet tastes
salty tastes

▲ **tongue**

top
1 the highest part of something
The vase is on top of the bookcase.
2 a toy that balances on a point and spins
Let's spin the top.
3 an item of clothing for the upper body
That's a pretty top.
4 a cover for a container, such as a box
Put the top back on the box.

tortoise
a land animal that can pull its head and legs into the shell that covers its body
Tortoises are very slow-moving animals.

▼ **tortoise**

touch (touching, touched)
1 to put your fingers or hand on something
Don't touch the paintings.
2 to be so close to another thing that there is no space between the two
The wires are touching.

towel
a cloth that you use to dry things or your body with
Dry your hands on the towel.

town
a place with houses and other buildings where people live and work
A town is smaller than a city.

toy
something that children like to play with
Can I play with my toy plane?

◀ **toy**

tractor
a big vehicle that is used on a farm
Tractors are very powerful.

traffic lights
where two or more roads meet, lights that change color, telling you when to stop and go
Turn left at the traffic lights.

▶ **traffic lights**

Tt

train
a line of cars pulled by an engine on a track
Trains travel at a fast speed.

▲ **train**

transport (transporting, transported)
to move people or things from one place to another
The tanker is transporting all the fuel

trap (trapping, trapped)
to catch something in a piece of equipment
It traps mice.

travel (traveling, traveled)
to go from one place to another
They're traveling by car.

treasure
a collection of valuable things
The chest is filled with treasure.

▲ **treasure**

tree
a large, tall plant with a trunk and branches
It's fun to climb trees.

trick
1 something done to entertain people
That was a clever trick.
2 something done to fool or cheat someone
That was a mean trick.

trip (tripping, tripped)
to catch your foot on something; to stumble
He tripped on the step.

trip
a journey
It's a short trip.

trouble
a problem or a worrying situation
We're having trouble with the new computer.

truck
a vehicle for carrying loads
We were stuck behind a truck.

trunk
1 the main part of a tree
Palm trees have tall trunks.
2 an elephant's nose
The elephant has a long trunk.
3 a box for storing things in.
Where's the key for this trunk?
4 part of a car for carrying things
The box is in the trunk

try (trying, tried)
1 to make an effort to do or get something
I tried to phone you.
2 to test or sample something
Have you tried the pasta?

turn
1 to move so you are looking or going in a new direction
He turned to look at us.
2 to move something to a different position
Turn the dial.

turtle
an animal that lives in water, which can pull its head and legs into the shell on its back
Turtles are good swimmers.

◄ **truck**

a b c d e f g h i j k l m

Uu

ugly
not nice to look at
What an ugly color!

umbrella
a piece of equipment made of cloth stretched over a frame that keeps the rain off
It's raining outside—I'll take my umbrella.

▲ umbrella

uncle
your mother's or father's brother; or your aunt's husband
He looks like his uncle.

under
below; to a lower place
Put your bag under your seat.

understand
(understanding, understood)
1 to know the meaning of words or ideas
Does he understand English?
2 to know how something works
Doctors understand the disease.
3 to know how and why someone feels or acts a certain way
You don't understand.

• Did you know? •
You can understand lots of words from other languages.
The English language has borrowed words from many other languages.
• From Italian, we have words like: balcony, giraffe, and violin.
• From Spanish, we have banana and guitar.
• From French, we have chocolate, crocodile, and medicine.

underwear
pieces of clothing that you wear next to your body under your other clothes
Pack some underwear.

unhappy
not happy; sad
Cheer up—try not to look so unhappy.

▶ unhappy

uniform
clothes worn by everyone in a group of people
Everyone wore uniforms.

▲ uniforms

up
toward a higher position
Pass that brush up to me.

upset
1 feeling worried, sad, or angry
I didn't mean to upset you.
2 feeling sick
His stomach is upset.

upstairs
toward or on the upper floors of a building
Take these papers upstairs.

Vv

valley
the low land between two hills
There is a river in the valley.

van
a small truck
The delivery van is here.

vanish (vanishing, vanished)
to disappear
The deer suddenly vanished.

vase
a container to hold flowers
The vase is hand-painted.

◀ vase

vegetable
a plant grown for food
Vegetables are healthy foods.

vehicle
a machine that carries people or things
Trucks and trains are vehicles.

velvet
a soft, thick material
My dress is made of red velvet.

vet (veterinarian)
an animal doctor
The vet is treating our dog.

◀ vet

videocassette recorder (VCR)
a machine for recording or playing TV shows
Turn on the VCR.

▲ VCR

village
a group of houses and buildings in the country
It's a beautiful old village.

vinegar
a liquid that is used to preserve food or add flavor
Add vinegar to the dressing.

violin
a musical instrument that is played with a bow
He's learning to play the violin.
▲ violin

virus (viruses)
1 a very tiny living thing that causes disease and illness
Flu is caused by a virus.
2 a computer program that can damage files
The virus has damaged my files.

visit (visiting, visited)
to go to see a person or a place
You can visit us this evening.

voice
the sounds a person makes when speaking or singing
I didn't recognize your voice.

volcano (volcanoes)
a mountain with an opening that sprays out steam or lava
The volcano is very active.

vote (voting, voted)
to show which idea or person you choose by raising your hand or writing on paper
Let's take a vote on this.

a b c d e f g h i j k l m

Ww

waiter

a man who serves food in a restaurant or café
Call the waiter and get the check.

▲ **waiter**

waitress

a woman who serves food in a restaurant or café
Ask the waitress for the check.

wake (waking, woke, woken)

to stop being asleep
Wake up!

walk (walking, walked)

to move along, putting one foot in front of the other.
Let's walk together

•Puzzle time•

There are six words that start with 'W' in this puzzle. Can you find all of them? Words are written vertically ↓ and horizontally →

a	b	c	d	w	e	f
a	b	c	w	a	l	k
a	b	w	i	n	c	d
w	h	i	s	t	l	e
a	b	c	h	d	e	f
v	a	b	c	d	e	f
e	a	b	c	d	e	f

answers
walk wave want whistle
win wish

wall

1 the side of a room or a building
There are several pictures on the wall.
2 a structure made of stone or brick that divides a space
There's a brick wall around the backyard.

wand

a magic stick that fairies, witches, and magicians use to do magic tricks
She waved her wand and turned the pumpkin into a coach.

want (wanting, wanted)

to wish, desire, or need something
Do you want a sandwich?

---

wardrobe

a piece of furniture to hang clothes in
It's a big wardrobe.

wash (washing, washed)

to clean with water
Wash your face with soap and water.

wasp

a black and yellow flying insect that stings
Wasps live in nests.

▲ **wasps**

wastebasket

a container to put unwanted paper and trash in
Empty the wastebasket.

watch

a small clock that you wear on your wrist
I'd like a watch for my birthday.

watch (watching, watched)

to look at something and pay attention
We're watching TV.

water

a liquid that falls from the sky as rain
Have a glass of water.

---

waterfall
water from a stream or a river that falls straight down over rocks
There is a pool under the waterfall.

▲ **waterfall**

wave
1 a raised part of moving water on the ocean
Waves crashed on the beach.
2 a movement of your hand to say goodbye, or hello, or to get someone's attention
Wave to your friends.
3 the way light and sound move
The sound of the music is carried on radio waves.

▼ **wave**

weak
not strong
I feel weak and dizzy.

wear (wearing, wore)
to have something, such as clothes, on your body
What should I wear to the party?

weather
the condition of the air—how hot or cold it is, the wind, rain and clouds
What's the weather like today?

web
1 the very thin threads a spider weaves
A spider catches food in its web.
2 the World Wide Web on the Internet
Do you use the Web?

Tarantulas are big, hairy spiders that live in hot countries. Their bite can kill small animals.

tarantula

How many words of three letters or more can you make from tarantula? You should be able to make at least 10.

week
seven days
See you next week!

weigh (weighing, weighed)
1 to measure how heavy something is
Weigh the fruit.
2 to be heavy or light
How much do you weigh?

well
1 in a good way
Well done!
2 healthy; not sick
Get well soon.

wet
not dry
Your hair's still wet.

whale
a very large sea animal
Whales are mammals, not fish.

▼ **whale**

wheel
a round object that turns and moves a vehicle along
The wheel came off the bike.

whisper (whispering, whispered)
to speak very quietly so other people can't hear
Whisper the secret to me.

whistle (whistling, whistled)

to blow air out through your lips and make a sound
Can you whistle?

wicked

very bad or evil
The wicked witch trapped them.

wife (wives)

the woman that a man is married to
His wife is very nice.

win (winning, won)

to be the first or the best in a race or other competition
He's won the race!

▲ **win**

wind

air moving across the ground
The wind is strong.

window

a glass-covered opening in a building
Look out the window.

winter

the time of year between fall and spring
The weather can be very cold in the winter.

▲ **winter**

wish (wishing, wished)

to hope for or want something
What did you wish for?

•Puzzle time•

Use the code to find out what someone has wished for

A	B	C	D	E	F	G	H	I	J
1	2	3	4	5	6	7	8	9	10

K	L	M	N	O	P	Q	R
11	12	13	14	15	16	17	18

S	T	U	V	W	X	Y	Z
19	20	21	22	23	24	25	26

1 14/5/23 2/9/11/5

answer
a new bike

witch (witches)

a woman who is supposed to have magical powers
The witches huddled over their big, black pot, making spells.

▲ **witches**

• Did you know? •

Witches have been around for thousands of years. Originally, witchcraft was an ancient religion. In the Middle Ages, many people were burned at the stake, accused of being witches. Modern witches do exist, but they do not fly on broomsticks!

wizard

a man who is supposed to have magical powers
The wizard broke the spell.

▲ **wizard**

wolf (wolves)

a wild animal that looks like a large dog
They heard the wolf howling at the moon.

▶ **wolf**

woman (women)

a female adult
Are there women working on the team?

wonder (wondering, wondered)

to think about something and why it is that way
I wonder why she said that.

wood

the material that a tree is made of
Put more wood on the fire.

wool

1 hair that grows on animals, such as sheep.
The wool is thick and warm.
2 thread made from this hair
My sweater is made of wool.

worry (worrying, worried)

to have the feeling that something bad might happen
You shouldn't worry, it's not a problem.

work (working, worked)

1 to do a job
My aunt works in a hospital
2 to run or operate smoothly
This machine is working properly now.

• Puzzle time •

See if you can match the workers with the things they need to do their jobs.

A	B
actor	paint
artist	theater
barber	menu
pilot	scissors
waiter	plane

answers
actor/theatre, artist/paint,
barber/scissors, pilot/plane,
waiter/menu

world

the Earth; the planet that we live on and everything that is on it
The Nile is the longest river in the world.

worm

a long, thin animal with no legs that lives in soil
Worms are good for the soil.

▲ **worm**

• Did you know? •

The Gippsland giant worm is a 13-foot-long (4-meters) Australian earthworm. It makes a slurping, gurgling sound as it slides its way through its burrow.

worse (worst)

see also bad
That is the worst song on the CD.

write (writing, wrote)

1 to make a new story, poem, play, song, or book
I wrote an exciting story at school.
2 to make letters, numbers, and words
Write your name in the book.

wrong

not right; incorrect
We took a wrong turn.

x-ray

1 a beam of energy that can go through solid things
X-rays are used at airports.
2 a photograph of the inside of the body
The x-ray shows that his hand may be broken.

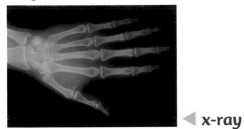
◀ **x-ray**

xylophone

a musical instrument that is played by hitting flat wooden or metal bars with a pair of sticks
The word xylophone comes from the Greek words "xylo" (wood) and "phone" (sound).

◀ **xylophone**

yacht

a boat with a sail
Let's go out on the yacht.

◀ **yacht**

yawn (yawning, yawned)

to open your mouth and take a deep breath, usually when you are tired or bored
I can't stop yawning—I'm going to bed.

year

a period of time that is equal to 12 months, especially from January to December
We're moving to a new house early next year.

yes

a word that is used to say that you want something, that you will do something, that you agree with something, or that something is true
Would you like another slice of pizza? Yes, please!

yesterday

the day before today
I phoned you yesterday.

yo-yo

a toy that moves up and down on a string that you hold in your hand
This yo-yo glows in the dark.

▼ **yo-yo**

yoga

exercises for your body and mind
Yoga comes from India.

yogurt

a food made from milk
I'd like some strawberry yogurt.

young

not old
The dog is still very young.

zebra

a wild black and white striped animal that looks like a horse
Zebras live in Africa.

▲ **zebras**

zero

nothing; 0
The temperature is zero degrees.

zipper

a fastener made of two rows of teeth that lock together
This case needs a new zipper.

zoo

a place where wild animals are kept so that people can look at them and study them
We went to the zoo.

Useful lists of words

Days of the week

Sunday
Monday
Tuesday
Wednesday
Thursday
Friday
Saturday

Months of the year

January
February
March
April
May
June
July
August
September
October
November
December

Numbers

1	one	first
2	two	second
3	three	third
4	four	fourth
5	five	fifth
6	six	sixth
7	seven	seventh
8	eight	eighth
9	nine	ninth
10	ten	tenth
11	eleven	eleventh
12	twelve	twelfth
13	thirteen	thirteenth
14	fourteen	fourteenth
15	fifteen	fifteenth
16	sixteen	sixteenth
17	seventeen	seventeenth
18	eighteen	eighteenth
19	nineteen	nineteenth
20	twenty	twentieth
21	twenty-one	twenty-first
22	twenty-two	twenty-second
23	twenty-three	twenty-third
24	twenty-four	twenty-fourth
25	twenty-five	twenty-fifth
26	twenty-six	twenty-sixth
27	twenty-seven	twenty-seventh
28	twenty-eight	twenty-eighth
29	twenty-nine	twenty-ninth
30	thirty	thirtieth
40	forty	fortieth
50	fifty	fiftieth
60	sixty	sixtieth
70	seventy	seventieth
80	eighty	eightieth
90	ninety	ninetieth
100	one hundred	hundredth
101	one hundred and one	one hundred and first
1,000	one thousand	thousandth
1,000,000	one million	millionth

Colors

red

orange

yellow

green

blue

indigo

violet

▲ **rainbow colors**

Shapes

triangle

circle

oval

square

rectangle

diamond

pentagon

hexagon

octagon

semicircle

Other colors we see and use

purple

pink

gray

cream

brown

white

black

turquoise

lilac

Measurements of length

inch (in)
foot (ft) = 12 in
yard (yd) = 3 ft
miles = 1,760 yd

Measurements of weight

ounce (oz)
pound (lb) = 16 oz
ton = 2,000 lb

Our world

North America

Europe

Asia

South America

Antarctica

Africa

Oceania

Time

o'clock
quarter past
half past
quarter to

of the clock
fifteen minutes past the hour
thirty minutes past the hour
fifteen minutes until the next hour

Seasons

Spring

Summer

Fall

Winter

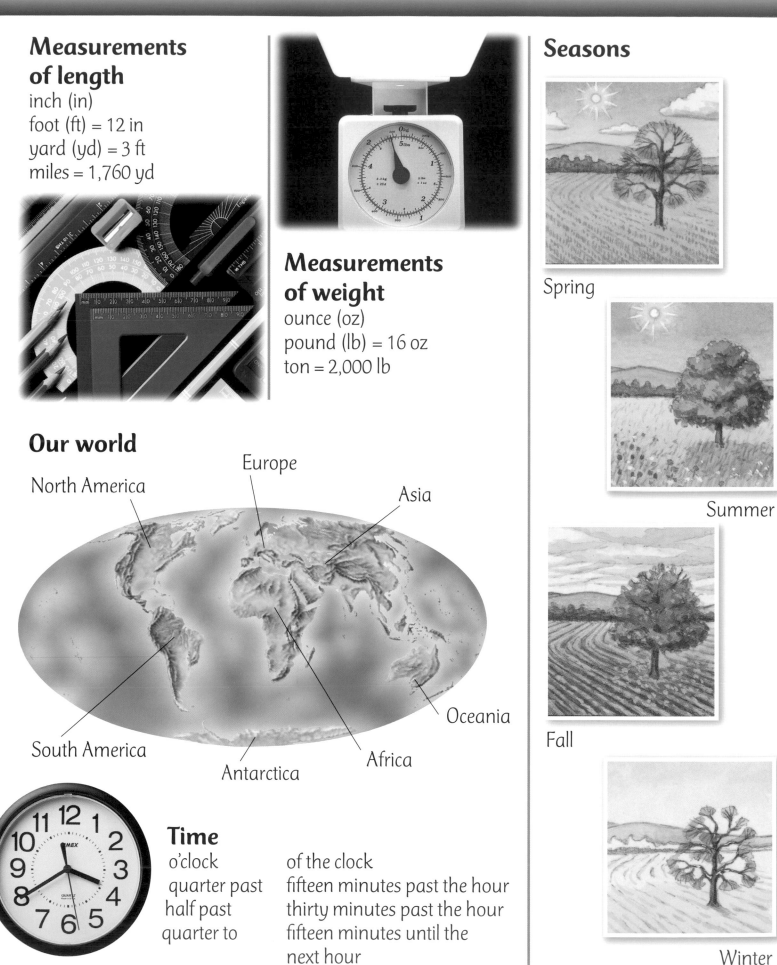

Words that we use all the time

Here is an alphabetical list of words you use all the time. This list will help you check your spelling.

Aa
accident
add
aeroplane
afraid
afternoon
again
airplane
also
angry
animal
another
answer
any
apple
asleep
away

Bb
baby
back
bad
bag
ball
balloon
bat
bath
beautiful
because
bed
begin
behind
below
between
bicycle
big
birthday
body
book
boy
bring
brother
build

Cc
cake
call
can
car
careful
cat
CD
cell phone
chair
change
chocolate
choice
climb
clock
close
clothes
coat
cold
color
computer
count

could
cry

Dd
dad
dance
daughter
day
die
difficult
dinner
dinosaur
disk
doctor
dog
door
down
draw
dress
drink
drive
dry

Ee
ear
early
easy
eat
egg
e-mail
end
enjoy
enough
except
eye

Ff
face
fall
family
far
faraway
farm
fast
feel
fill
find
fire
floor
follow
food
football
forget
forward
free
friend
frighten
front
fruit
full
fun
funny

Gg
garden
ghost
girl

give
good
good-bye
great
grow

Hh
hair
hamburger
hand
happen
happy
hate
head
hear
heavy
hello
help
here
hide
high
hill
hit
hold
holiday
home
homework
hope
horrible
hospital
hot
hour
hungry
hurry
hurt

Ii
ice
ice cream
idea
important
inside
interesting
Internet
its
it's (it is)

Jj
jacket
jam
job
join
joke
juice
jump
jumper
just

Kk
keep
kettle
key
keyboard
kick
kill
kiss

kitchen
know
knew

Ll
lamp
large
last
late
laugh
learn
leave
let
library
lie
light
like
listen
little
long
look
loose
lose
loud
love
lovely
lucky
lunch

Mm
machine
magic
make
man
mean
meat
medicine
meet
middle
milk
minute
mirror
miss
mom
money
monitor
monster
more
morning
move
much
music
must

Nn
name
naughty
near
never
new
news
next
nice
night
nobody
noise
none
no one
nothing
now
number

Oo
off
often
OK (okay)
old
once
open
ordinary
out
outdoor
over
own

Pp
pack
page
pain
paint
pair
paper
park
part
party
pass
passed
past
pay
pen
pencil
person
pet
phone
photo
picture
piece
place
plane
play
playground
please
police
pool
poor
present
pretend
pretty
price
printer
problem
pull
puppy
push
put

Qq
quarter
queen
question
quick
quickly
quiet
quite
quilt

Rr
race
radio
rain
read
remember
remind
repeat

rest
return
rich
ride
right
ring
road
room
run

Ss
sad
safe
same
sandwich
school
screen
sea
secret
see
send
shape
shoe
shout
show
shut
sing
sister
sit
sky
sleep
slow
smart
smile
sneeze
snow
socks
some
song
sorry
spell
stand
start
stay
stop
store
story
strong
suddenly
sun
surprise
swim

Tt
table
take
talk
tall
tea
teacher
teddy bear
telephone
television (TV)
tell
thank
their
there
think
thought
through
tired
together

toilet
top
touch
toy
trash
tree
try

Uu
ugly
umbrella
under
understand
unhappy
uniform
up
upset
upstairs

Vv
van
VCR
vegetable
village
visit
voice

Ww
wake
walk
wall
want
warm
wash
watch
water
wave
weather
week
weigh
well
wet
wheel
whisper
who's (who is)
whose
win
wind
window
wish
wonder
wood
work
world
would
write
wrong

XxYyZz
x-ray
yawn
year
yes
yesterday
young
zebra
zipper
zoo

The publishers would like to thank the following artists who have contributed
to this book:

Lisa Alderson, Julie Banyard, Martin Camm, Jim Channell,
Kuo Kang Chen, Mark Davis, Nicholas Forder, Mike Foster, Luigi Gallante,
Peter Gregory, Alan Hancocks, Ron Haywood, Sally Holmes, Richard Hook,
Rob Jakeway, Tony Kenyon, Sue King, Steve Kirk, Mick Loates, Kevin Madison,
Alan Male, Janos Marffy, Josephine Martin, Tracy Morgan, Gill Platt, Terry Riley, Andy Robinson,
Mike Saunders, Peter Sarson, Rob Sheffield, Guy Smith, Roger Smith,
Mike Taylor, Peter Taylor, Mike White, Colin Woolf

The publishers would like to thank Ted Smart for the generous loan of his illustrations

The publishers would like to thank the following for supplying photographs for this book:
Corbis: Reuters New Media 133 (c/l)

All other pictures from the Miles Kelly Archives